We Need Each Other

We Need Each Other

Reaching Deeper Levels
in Our Interpersonal Relationships

Guy Greenfield

BAKER BOOK HOUSE

Grand Rapids, Michigan 49506

To
Fish and Ruby Greenfield,
parents who gave me my first lessons
in relationships
through faith, hope and love

Contents

Foreword

In this book Guy Greenfield speaks to all of us at the point of our deepest needs. Indeed, we are spiritual beings, but we are much more. To be rightly related to God is the basis for all relationships, but it is only the starting point. Those relationships must be developed to the ultimate. Our Lord's statement, "Thou shalt love the Lord thy God with all thy heart, and with all thy soul, and with all thy strength, and with all thy mind; and thy neighbor as thyself," is the most comprehensive psychological statement ever made.

This book will be read primarily by Christians who are rightly related to God and who are making steady progress in the pursuit of being rightly related to themselves. But few of us know much about how we can consistently, analytically, and determinedly pursue building truly meaningful relationships with others.

How many true friends do we have? How well do we really know our neighbors, our business associates, even our children and spouses? Probably less than 10 percent is known of the wonderful person who is actually there. We make small talk, we exchange cheerful greetings, we pretend to be interested, but little more. To know and be known, to give and receive love at the deepest levels of human communication, give life its richest meaning beyond that fellowship with God which is its basis.

In *We Need Each Other*, Guy Greenfield has spoken masterfully, even

9

profoundly, on this critical issue. He insightfully declares, "Just as our physical bodies suffer from a nutritional deficiency when we do not consume adequate amounts of vitamins, minerals, and various nutrients, so will our personalities suffer from a relational deficiency when we do not consume the support that comes from meaningful relationships. A hungry body will send out danger signals called hunger pains and eventually a neglected body will produce signs of illness and disease (dis-ease). Likewise, a deprived spirit will give out its danger signals: negative, critical, judgmental words and behavior. The person who complains a lot is telling us that he has a relational deficiency." All of us need to recognize that we "will find relational sufficiency only at the deeper levels" of our interpersonal relationships.

Read the first chapter and you will not be able to put this book down. Listen, really listen, with your soul to what these pages are saying. This is a book that could change the world!

John R. Bisagno, Pastor
First Baptist Church
Houston, Texas

Preface

This book is the product of several years of observation, experience, and reflection as a pastor, as a sociology teacher on the college level, as a pastor again, and now as a Christian ethics teacher on a graduate seminary level. I could not have written this particular book without these more than thirty years of experience.

The church and the classroom have taught me several important things, including the significance of relationships and human emotions, that I did not and could not gain from my early academic training. If there are any serious weaknesses or gaps in the lives of Christians in general and in the training of church leaders in particular they are in these two areas of experience.

As a teacher of ethics, I am doubly convinced that there is an inextricable connection between one's moral behavior and the two areas of relationships and emotions. Belief and thinking are very important in Christian living, but we dare not, except to our great loss, neglect the nature and quality of relationships and feelings or else Christian living will be sorely vulnerable to setback or defeat.

Although I discuss emotions in the pages that follow, my emphasis is upon relationships, primarily identifying and analyzing levels of relating. My first goal is showing how desperately in home, church, and society *we need each other*.

I have tried to avoid using technical academic or professional jar-

gon. Some of the anecdotes I use are very personal. At the same time
that I have tried to make this book personal, practical, and enjoyable,
I have tried to say something of substance to challenge the reader to
think and to decide. My second goal is that you will find some paths
to help you deepen your own relationships and enrich your own life.

I am indebted to many people for making this book possible: the
congregations I have served, the students I have taught, and primarily
my family. I refer often to my wife of thirty-one years. Without Carole
this book could not and would not have been possible. She was a
constant source of encouragement through all of its stages.

I want to express special appreciation to President Russell H. Dil-
day, Jr., Provost John P. Newport, and Theology Dean William Tolar,
my administrative superiors at Southwestern Baptist Theological
Seminary, Fort Worth, Texas, for their support and encouragement to
use my summer away from teaching to produce this book. To the
members of the Education Commission of the Southern Baptist Con-
vention for their provision of a postdoctoral research grant, I express
my deepest gratitude for their confidence. I also wish to express special
appreciation to Linda Triemstra, my project editor at Baker Book
House, for her superb editing of the manuscript. Her several suggestions and improvements have made the book more readable and
understandable.

Finally, I want to express my heartfelt thanks to Principal Barrie
White of Regent's Park College of Oxford University and his faculty
and staff for their exceptional hospitality to me as a postdoctoral research student. Particularly helpful was their provision of a place to
research and write in the Regent's Park College library. "For the gifts
of your grace and the fellowship of this college, we thank you, O God."

Guy Greenfield
At Regent's Park College
Oxford University
Oxford, U.K.
Trinity Term, 1983

Introduction

How many close friends do you have? I mean really *close*? Do you have even *one*? I'm talking about the kind of person who understands you, cares about you, listens to you, accepts and values you the way you are, doesn't have any specific plans for your improvement, isn't trying to use you for personal gain, has your best interests at heart, is available at three in the morning if needed, can be trusted with five thousand dollars of your cash, respects your religious and political views even if different from his or hers, and, most significant of all symbolically and practically, whose face lights up when you come into the room.

Do such people actually exist? I certainly hope so. I would like to be that kind of person, and, furthermore, I need a few people like this in my life. We need each other. We really do.

Life is too short to "go it alone." Aren't you tired of being lonely, living in a sort of crowded isolation, busying yourself in all kinds of bustle with lots of people but passing as ships in the night? I have learned that I am a social being in need of others, not an independent person but an interdependent one. I was born in a social matrix, and I was created to live in a social environment where others are as important to my welfare and happiness as are food, water, air, and safety. There are those to whom I must say in all honesty, "I need you, and you need me." We need each other.

I could not have become a human being without other human beings. I could not have developed as a maturing, productive, useful human being without the help of other humans, particularly my family, teachers, peers, and other members of my community.

However, somewhere in this process of human growth and development something usually goes wrong. Let's call it a cultural problem. But what is culture? The sociologist defines culture as all the accumulated norms, values, beliefs, symbols, and material products of a society. In other words, culture provides us all with a script to tell us how to act on the stage of life.

Distance and Loneliness

The problem is that, at least in American culture, part of that script says, "Don't get too close to anyone, keep your distance, play it cool, or you might get hurt." Mix that with heavy doses of individualism, a rigid work ethic, and an estimate of human value that is based largely upon personal performance, and you can end up in a rather lonely existence.

Loneliness is undoubtedly a factor in much of the mental illness and behavioral problems in contemporary society. However you describe loneliness—alienation, isolation, or the feeling of being cut off from others—humans simply cannot cope with it, because humans need each other. The worst form of punishment in prison is solitary confinement. Administrators of the space-exploration program recognized early that they did not dare send a lone man into space for long. Suicides tend to be people who felt isolated or had broken ties with significant others. Note the high suicide rates among college youth who are away from home and friends, and the elderly whose mate has died or whose work associates and friends have retired.

Loneliness is definitely related to the problem of distance ("don't get too close to anyone"). Too many of us were taught, mostly indirectly, not to touch other people. Never hug. Never embrace. Never kiss in public. Don't put your arm around anyone. Keep your distance. It's all right to talk about love and affection, but don't express it. Consequently, many people reach their adult years and do not feel loved by anyone, yet they may be married and have several children! Where did we get such crazy ideas?

The Need for Closeness

Social-science practitioners generally agree that most of the problems related to crime and delinquency are directly related to the lack of love and closeness in the lives of offenders. The cultural requirement of maintaining distance is like telling people they need air but just be sure to breathe as little as possible!

A human infant who is mechanically fed and changed and yet never held, touched, cuddled, or spoken to in loving tones, will die in a short time. Food, air, and cleanliness are not enough. Older humans (children, teen-agers, and adults) need love also. They need closeness, touching, affection, and careful attention as persons of worth and significance. Without such treatment, they will behave in all sorts of abnormal and destructive ways. When will we ever learn this?

Even churches are affected by the impersonality of society. During my seminary training we were warned: "Never touch a member of the congregation, especially someone of the opposite sex." Naturally, handshaking was the only exception. It's interesting that in American culture shaking hands is a symbolic way both of greeting others and of maintaining one's distance. How different from the biblical injunction to greet one another with a holy kiss (Rom. 16:16; 1 Cor. 16:20; 2 Cor. 13:12; 1 Thess. 5:26)! During most of my years as a Christian I never hugged anyone and very few ever hugged me. This has changed in recent years but not nearly enough.

It seems strange that one of the biblical stories often told in churches portrays the father of the prodigal son as one who "embraced and kissed" his returning son (read Luke 15:11–32, especially v. 20). The usual interpretation is that the father's behavior symbolizes the behavior of God himself. Another story tells of early Christians weeping, embracing, and kissing Paul as they bid him farewell (Acts 20:37). Why is this kind of behavior now taboo?

If you can't get close to people in the church, with whom can you be close?

The Need for Relational Theology

Relationships are what this book is all about. This is not a book about theology, but it is based upon what might be called relational theology. Actually, the only kind of Christian theology I care anything about is relational theology. God coming in Jesus Christ to reconcile sinners to himself and to unite a new community of believers into a fellowship of ministry sounds pretty relational to me. To describe the church as "the family of God" implies that the church ought to provide its members with the opportunity to be involved in ongoing, close relationships.

It is so easy to get away from this goal even in the name of biblical theology. A friend of mine, a theology professor, once told me about receiving a letter from a former colleague of his who had moved to a new teaching position some months before. They had taught together for several years and considered each other a friend. However, my friend had written an article for a professional journal and his former colleague had written to chide and challenge him on certain points in the article.

My friend commented to me, "Isn't it interesting that in this first letter from him since moving to his new position not one word in five pages was expressed in any personal way, no questions about my wife and children, and no comments about his own family. It was all business, and theology at that." I would call this the heresy of nonrelational theology. Theology that emphasizes ideas to the neglect of relationships is simply bad theology—cold, aloof, and certainly not Christian in the finest biblical sense.

Levels of Relating

For the past several years I have given attention to the observation, study, and experiencing of relationships in a variety of settings: marriage and family, church, work, and friendship circles. This book is an attempt to share what I have learned. I have discovered eight levels of relating,[1] from the shallowest to the deepest (see Fig. 1).

I have discovered that most people operate on several levels simultaneously, depending upon the who, what, when, where, and why of their contacts with a variety of people. Also, as one moves from the shallower levels to the deeper levels the number of people one relates to becomes smaller.

I have also noticed that problems arise when people never or rarely move past level 5 (social interaction) with anyone. In my observations,

1. Some people might argue that "relating" is the wrong word and that "associating" or "association" would be preferable. However, I am trying to stress progression toward deeper emotional levels and an attitude resembling that shared by relatives. Therefore, I prefer the term *relating* to the word *associating*.

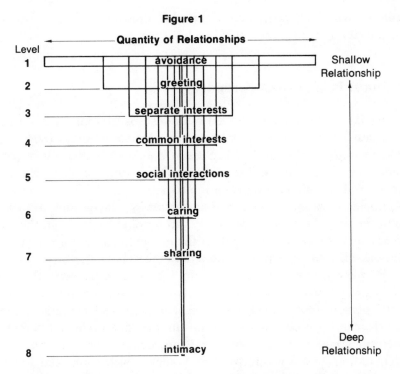

Figure 1

I found that few people move into levels 6, 7, or 8 with anyone—at least not for long or with much intensity. The basic problem experienced in remaining at level 5 is what I call the development of relational deficiency, which results in a judgmental attitude. This will be discussed in detail later. For now, let it be said that many people who are unhappy, critical, complaining, and judgmental are people suffering from relational deficiency. They will find relational sufficiency only at the deeper levels.

The descriptions of these eight levels of relationships can be applied to several types of friendship situations where ongoing relationships are involved: marriage (the relationship of husband and wife); family (the relationships of parents and children and other relatives with each other); work (relationships with one's associates and business or professional contacts); community (relationships with one's neighbors and friends); church (relationships with fellow members in the context of church life and activities); and organizations (clubs, fraternities, sororities, and other formal associations in the community).

Actually, the descriptions are applicable whenever humans are in contact with each other over a period of time and with any degree of regularity.

Groups: Primary and Secondary

Social scientists have studied relationships for many years. One of the best-known studies was by Charles Horton Cooley (1864–1929). His findings were published in *Social Organization*, which is now considered a classic in the discipline. Cooley distinguished between primary and secondary groups within society.

Cooley's primary groups include the family, play-groups of children, and the neighborhood (community) group of elders. Within these immediate, intimate groups, within the context of their values and traditions, the child's earliest experiences take place.

Primary groups are essentially small groups, characterized by face-to-face relationships of an unspecialized nature. Group members are total persons (not a mere customer or patient) seeking satisfaction of all their many needs and aspirations in their day-to-day relationships. Relationships in these groups tend to become intense, intimate, and demanding, and are relatively permanent, even somewhat involuntary, especially in the family (you don't choose your parents).

Secondary groups are those larger associations that are formally organized and impersonal, in which membership is for some specific purpose only and largely voluntary.

Sociologists describe emotional relationships in similar terms. Primary relations are close, intimate, intense, personal, long-standing, and very formative and influential on one's growth and development. Examples are the relationship between husband and wife or parent and child.

Secondary relationships are distant, impersonal, structured, utilitarian, short-lived, and not too influential upon one's personality or behavior. Illustrations are the customer-clerk, employer-employee, or teacher-student relationships, especially in large, complex organizations or settings. Relationships in today's church unfortunately tend to be secondary, which causes some major problems and limitations for the contemporary Christian.

Remember that as one moves from level 1 toward level 8, one is moving from secondary to primary relationships. Therefore, it is important for one to move toward the deeper levels if one desires to engage in life-changing and personality-strengthening experiences.

Christian Living

A thesis of this book is that only at the deeper levels of relating will Christians discover the necessary motivation (the power, will, or strength) for living the Christian ethic: that is, the Christian life in all its dimensions, especially one's motives and consequent behavior. Living the Christian life is a matter not merely of *knowing* what is the right thing to do, but also of having the necessary motivation to do the right. Such motivation is more likely to be found at the deeper levels of relating than at the shallow levels.

Christian living flows best out of one's relationships (with God and others), which include the full range of human emotions, and not merely out of one's beliefs or thoughts. I *know* much better than I *do*. If my beliefs and thoughts can affect my behavior, and my behavior can affect my relationships, then my relationships can also affect my behavior which in turn can be affected by beliefs and thoughts. The church has historically tended to stress belief and thought, with some emphasis on behavior, but has neglected to emphasize the importance of relationships. In this book I attempt to correct this imbalance and emphasize the significance of relationships, especially those on the deeper levels.

I have found that life's most meaningful experiences are discovered only at the deeper levels of relating. This has been true in my marriage, in my role as a parent, and in the fellowship of a small group of Christians in a local church.

On one occasion, when Jesus said to Simon Peter, "Put out into the deep water, and let down the nets for a catch" (Luke 5:4, NIV), the men caught so many fish that two boats could not hold the catch. This is not simply another miracle story for us to read and be amazed by. It also serves to suggest that life's greatest discoveries are to be found at the deeper levels of experience and not in the shallows.

Reading a book is no substitute for experience, but I believe it is helpful for one to know that there are eight levels of relating and to discover how far one has gone in depth, how much further one needs to go, and how to get there.

It will be especially helpful if this book is read and discussed in a small group (not more than twelve people) of friends, family members, or fellow church members. After all, a study of relationships can best be done in the context of relationships!

I trust that this book will serve as a guide to enable you to find greater meaning in life at the deeper levels of relating.

Portrait of a friend

Consider this portrait of a friend:
When things don't come out right, he comes right in.
When none of your dreams come true, she remains true.
He never looks for your money except when you've lost it.
She never gets in your way except to clear it for you.
Nothing is more important to him than making you important.
She's in your corner when you are cornered.
He turns up when you get turned down.
All she wants in return for her helping hand is your handshake.
He never insists on seeing you except when nobody else wants to.
The only way she sponges off you is to absorb some of your troubles.
When you're taking bows, he bows out.
You can do anything you want with her friendship except buy it—
    or sell it.
He makes you realize that having a real friend is like having an
    extra life.
All she asks of your friendship is the privilege of deserving it.

Adapted from
James Pleitz, Pastor
Park Cities Baptist Church
Dallas, Texas

1

How Deep Are Your Relationships?

Until I married, I never really felt very close to anyone. The closest friend I had was, I suppose, my mother. My father, who was always cordial and good to me, seemed consumed in his work most of the time. My brother and sister were several years older than I. Oh, I had friends among my peers, but those were primarily social friendships. We seldom if ever talked about anything serious. Even the subject of girls was fun talk. In those days, talk about religion was out of the question. That was a family matter or a subject discussed only at church on Sunday, and when it was discussed it tended to be restricted to doctrinal matters (e.g., why do Methodists sprinkle and Baptists immerse?). It was never a theological or a personal question.

Marriage changed that, although not immediately. It was several years before my wife and I became the close friends we are today. So much of our early married life was consumed in schoolwork, the church (I was a pastor), and in time children (you know, diapers, dishes, and debts—the 3-D of early marriage). Through several years of growing, struggling, searching, and adjusting, my wife and I began to discover the meaning of depth in our relationship. Once we discovered the meaning of depth, we began to apply that knowledge to our other relationships.

How deep are your relationships? I am not suggesting that all of your relationships should have the greatest possible depth. My observation of the eight levels of relating reveals that most of our relationships will not have a great deal of depth. We have neither the time nor the opportunity to develop closeness. However, I am suggesting that we need to achieve significant, deep relationships with some people—whether one, a dozen, or twenty.

The Depth Factor

What do I mean by depth? All metaphors have their limitations, but by using the adjective *deep* I am describing a relationship that is meaningful and significant. A deep relationship is one in which two people develop a feeling of closeness. By closeness I mean mutual understanding, awareness, rapport, communion, and a feeling of oneness or togetherness. The opposite would be a shallow relationship—one that is distant, superficial, trivial, insignificant, empty of meaning. In a shallow relationship, people lack understanding of each other's innermost feelings and thoughts.

The Need for Closeness

Humans need closeness to one or more other people because it was through closeness that each of us became a human being. Do we ever forget that primary experience of living our first nine months inside the body of our mother? Our fetal home provided us with warmth, nourishment, and a sense of security, acceptance, and love. If closeness gave these important things to us in the beginning, it seems only natural to continue looking for them in closeness. We need closeness if we are going to continue receiving love, acceptance, security, and encouragement (which is psychological nourishment). This kind of closeness is, of course, more than physical. It is primarily emotional.

Closeness is also needed because it brings a sense of worth. I am of value to the person with whom I am close. Closeness brings a feeling of being understood. It is vital for me to know that at least one person in the world understands me. Closeness brings a feeling of being cared about. I can face the challenges of most any day when I know that at least one person in my life cares about me.

People who have no closeness, no depth in any of their relationships tend to be people who are unhappy, lonely, critical, uncooperative, even sometimes hostile, mean, and destructive. Suicidal people are rarely close to anyone. I am convinced that a lot of physical illness is symptomatic of people who are unloved, uncared for, lonely, and cut off from nurturing relationships.

People whose relationships tend to be shallow rarely make any meaningful contribution to anyone's life. They tend to be preoccupied with themselves and their own concerns. People who generally maintain an aloofness in their relationships are usually uninvolved in other people's problems and retain a rather self-centered lifestyle. These are not people-helpers. They are people-avoiders.

The Hunger for Closeness

A few years ago, as I was becoming aware of my need for closeness, I began developing a hunger for depth in my relationships. I really can't explain it, but I was tired of living in the shallows. I had many of the symptoms of trying to survive on superficial relationships: loneliness, insecurity, emptiness, faultfinding, certain psychosomatic illnesses, and self-centeredness.

My wife and I, fortunately for us at about the same time, began reaching out for something deeper than we had ever known. What caused us to do this? Several things, actually. But one very important weekend experience started us on our search. We met some people who had depth. They shared their inmost thoughts, feelings, aspirations, and joys. Our inclination was to reciprocate. And that started our search for deep relationships.

If you also sense the need for closeness, recognize that it can become a reality in your life, and know that other people around you are eager for depth in their lives too and are waiting for you to take the initiative.

The hunger for closeness may be related to your relationship to God. Maybe you've been a Christian for a while and have been making some progress in spiritual growth, but feel you've reached a plateau. Maybe your next step in spiritual growth is to discover depth and closeness in your relationships with some of the people nearest you. Maybe it will be in those deeper interpersonal relationships that God wants to meet you in a way you've never known Him heretofore. An awareness of that possibility could stimulate a new hunger for closeness.

The Fear of Closeness

By this time your anxiety level may be rising. Maybe you tried to get close to someone in the past and you "got burned." You possibly were disappointed, rebuffed, or even rejected. Or, maybe you're afraid that will happen.

Avoiding closeness is a way to avoid getting hurt. There is always an element of risk involved in searching for deeper relationships. For example, a very successful insurance executive—a husband and father, a deacon in his church—once told me that he would never try to get close to anyone. He said the risks were too great. It was strange that he ran a lot of risks in his business but never in his personal relationships. No wonder that his wife and daughters considered him a very distant person. He was a good provider materially and financially but not emotionally and affectionately. He was afraid of his emotions.

You may be afraid to let another person get close to you, because if he or she finds out about your real self and doesn't like what he or she learns, then rejection is final. It seems safer to keep your distance and pretend you're someone you're not.

For some American men, closeness is something to avoid, because others may learn of their inner fears and weaknesses. Men, says the culture, should never admit a weakness. And they do pay dearly for this cultural advice: shortened life span, poor health, weak marriages.

If you are afraid of depth and closeness in your relationships, think about the alternatives. The dangers of shallowness and distance seem more fearsome to me.

The Barriers to Closeness

Most of the barriers to achieving closeness are put up by the culture we live in. Some of these barriers have already been mentioned (e.g., men aren't supposed to let anyone get close to them). Another is the "don't touch" syndrome, which is a part of the Puritan attitude about sex and the human body. However, let's not blame the Puritans for all of this. Among men this rule about not touching is related to our deep fears of possible homosexual tendencies. And isn't it interesting that in our society the bumper sticker "Have you hugged your kid today?" appeared! Why would such a question even be asked? Because there is a hang-up about hugging on the part of many parents, but there is also a great need!

Evangelist Bill Glass, a former professional football player and a giant of a man, had finished preaching to a gathering of inmates at the Ellis Unit (maximum security) of the Texas Department of Corrections, when a convicted killer, a large man himself and considered one of the most dangerous in the unit, approached Bill and asked if he would talk with him. The inmate briefly told his life story and then asked, "Would you do me a favor? Would you hug me? I've been in here over twenty-five years and ain't no one hugged me in over twenty-five years."

Bill responded, "Sure, fellow, I'll hug you," and the two huge men gave each other a good long hug. In a few minutes, Bill invited the man to give his life to Jesus Christ, which the man did as the two knelt together in prayer. Later, Bill said he believed he actually hugged that man into the kingdom of God. There is great power in hugging. We desperately need to recover the power of its closeness.

Another barrier is the cultural idea that you aren't supposed to get personal with anyone. Personal matters are too private to share outside of the family. Why? Where did an idea like that get started? Maybe it began in the primitive belief that if you know something intimate about someone then you have power over that person. In biblical times there was a common belief that to know someone's name was to have power over him or her (possibly this belief is reflected in Luke 8:30, "What is your name?").

Have you ever heard a minister, about to give an illustration in a sermon, say, "Please excuse this personal reference"? What is wrong with getting personal? Personal stories make the best illustrations. One way for a preacher to add some life and depth to his sermons is to open up and share discriminatingly his inmost feelings and experiences. Yet the culture considers that taboo.

A major barrier to closeness and depth in our relationships is the nature of our modern urban lifestyle: too busy, too crowded, too materialistic. To develop close relationships takes time, a reordering of one's priorities, and a commitment to find depth. It requires focusing our attention on a few people rather than the masses. It calls for going out of our way to find those of like mind and with similar concerns for closeness. It means swimming against the current of today's urban style of living. But it can be done, and it's worth it.

By facing up to these barriers to closeness, maybe we can recognize them for what they are and work to overcome them.

The Depth Factor at Work in Levels of Relating

As we move in our relationships from levels 1 to 8, we are moving into progressively deeper relationships. We usually move consecutively from one level to another, although sometimes we may by-pass the shallowest levels (e.g., if we are appointed to a committee). It is also important to recognize that the number of people we can relate to diminishes as we go deeper. This is natural and to be expected. We have neither the time nor the emotional energy to relate to as many people on the deeper levels as we do on the shallower levels. I will now list again the eight levels of relating in order to explain how the depth factor works in them.

Level one: the avoidance level. There are two possibilities here: one positive or neutral; the other negative. Quite normally we avoid relating to most people we meet. These are the many people we pass on the street or in the halls of a building. We do not know them. If we recognize any of them, we do not have either time or opportunity to speak. These people we avoid unintentionally. Conversely, the negative type of avoidance involves those people we do not like for some reason or another. Maybe they once said or did something offensive to us. They may be rude or obnoxious people to whom we would rather not even speak. We intentionally avoid them. This is the shallowest of all the levels. Essentially, little if any relating takes place.

Level two: the greeting level. On the greeting level we at least acknowledge each other with some kind of greeting: a spoken hello, a smile, or a nod. We recognize the presence and, possibly, the identity of each other. This is better than being ignored. A greeting meets the basic universal human need to be recognized.

Level three: the separate-interests level. When we go deeper than the greeting level, we begin probing to see if perchance we have anything in common. With some people we find that we have only separate interests. Our backgrounds, experiences, and tastes are sufficiently different that our conversations tend to reach a dead end. Because we have little if anything in common, the relationship could die of disinterest. Having anything in common is often a matter of degree. Unless people can find at least some common interests, the relationship is not likely to thrive. (It doesn't have to be that way, but it probably will be.) Most people have difficulty developing a close relationship if there aren't some common interests.

Level four: the common-interests level. If we discover that we have some common interests, then our relationship will probably deepen. Our conversations will deal with matters of mutual commitment, concern, and investment.

For example, if we find that both of us are Christians, belong to the same religious denomination, are from the same hometown or state, have children of the same approximate age, agree somewhat on current political or economic issues, or like to fish, hunt, or ski, then we are likely to build a relationship on these commonalities.

We grow closer through our common interests, and we are likely to identify with each other. Common interests serve as the bridges that often bring strangers together. This level of relating, however, is only a conversational level, as is the separate-interests level. At these levels people merely share ideas in the search for friendship. Feelings are not a major part of the relationship.

Level five: the social-interaction level. Once we have discovered some common interests, this initial attraction may lead us to affiliate in some way and begin doing things together. Social interaction means that two or more people engage in a common activity.

For instance, we may serve on the same committee at church or civic club; we may work together as a team in sports or community service; we may attend a movie together; we may decide to play tennis or jog together. Our common interests provide the opportunity to share these activities beyond the conversational stage. Common talk produces common walk. Our common interests become common activities, and social interaction takes us deeper into our relationship. We now talk about not merely what we think but also what we do together.

This level can produce something of a crisis. A crisis can be defined as a stage in a sequence of events at which the trend of all future events is determined; that is, a turning point. At the social-interaction level, we may discover that we really don't care for, like, or prefer each other, and consequently revert to a shallower level, even the avoidance level. We may find that our common interests and activities are not in themselves sufficient reasons to stay together. Perhaps our personalities clash. Possibly our differences, undetected earlier, outweigh our similarities. Our interests may be the same but our values or goals in life differ.

Level six: the caring level. Relationships take a new direction if and when this level is reached. Moving from level 5 to level 6 is a major step in any relationship. One must decide to shift away from being self-centered to reach the caring level. Caring involves being aware of and sensitive to others' needs and situations and getting directly involved in their lives.

To care means to listen, to learn, to reach out, and to make yourself available. It may or may not call for material or financial assistance, but it will call for *you* as a person through genuine encouragement and affirmation. If you truly care for someone, you cannot help but get very close to that person. I have noticed that the students who share with me the details of a serious personal problem and give me an opportunity to care for them in some direct, even tangible, way are the students with whom I am most likely to develop closeness.

When I was a college sociology teacher, a ministerial student asked me to help him with his degree plan. He had been poorly advised and his degree plan was the biggest mess I'd ever seen. The young man was extremely despondent, for it looked to him like it would take "forever" to graduate. I went to work on the plan, consulted with the dean, made some substitutions, rearranged the student's schedule, and enabled him to graduate much sooner than he expected. His new degree plan was like a map out of the woods of academia. Now, some fifteen years after our initial contact, he is a prominent staff member of a national missions board. Mike Wilson often visits our seminary campus and, when he does, comes by my office just to talk. To this day, when we see each other, our faces light up! Caring produces depth and closeness.

Level seven: the sharing level. Among some of those about whom you can meaningfully care, you can find some with whom you can share. This is not simply sharing your money or possessions or time where there is a real need. That should happen on level 6. The sharing level is where you open up, become vulnerable, run some risks, and reveal the true and honest *you*. The thought of honest self-disclosure scares some people. It requires a good measure of trust and a willingness to run the risk of being rejected or disappointed.

Naturally, you have to be selective in choosing those people to whom you open yourself. It seems best to start with those few whom you perceive to be your best friends. A married couple could certainly start with each other. Sharing involves more than being nice and friendly. It means being honest. You move quickly from discussing facts, ideas, and information to talking about feelings, even one's deepest emotions.

Sharing does not call for hanging out all your dirty laundry of the past. Sharing calls for honesty about feelings, experiences (positive and negative), goals, dreams, victories and defeats, ups and downs of the *present*. This is the "who I am" and "where I am" of the here and now.

People with whom you can share your inner self will be people who will reciprocate. There won't be many of these truly close confidants—

ordinarily one to half a dozen. Some unusual people might find a dozen through the years. We are not emotionally equipped to relate to many more than that during each stage of the life cycle.

We need these mutual relationships for several reasons (to be discussed later). But recognize that relationships at this level provide us with mirrors that allow us to see ourselves and to help others close to us see themselves. We really can't find ourselves without other people. Cordiality alone won't do. We need to share our deepest feelings which lie at the heart of our personalities.

Level eight: the intimacy level. Intimacy is the deepest level of all. There will be very few to whom we will relate on this level in our entire lifetime. This level is very difficult to describe. To understand intimacy, you really need to experience it. One of the dictionary definitions of intimacy refers to sexual intercourse. That can be a very intimate experience between two people who deeply love each other, but it can also be mechanical and impersonal, simply a physical act. So I am using the term *intimate* to mean much more than something physical. This level of relating is actually a nonverbal, nonphysical, emotional and psychic experience. I could even use the word *spiritual*, because humans have a spirit.

The apostle Paul mentions the human spirit in the question, "For who among men knows the thoughts of a man except the man's spirit within him?" (1 Cor. 2:11, NIV; see also 1 Thess. 5:23). The phrase *man's spirit* refers to man's capacity to respond to God, the Holy Spirit, in that deepest of all relationships (see Luke 23:46; 1 Cor. 6:17). Is it possible that Paul was referring to the human spirit when he mentioned "the inner man" (Eph. 2:15, RSV) and "our inner nature" (2 Cor. 4:16, RSV)? When two human spirits are in communion with each other, they are at the intimacy level.

Those most likely to experience intimacy are a husband and wife who, in time, develop a closeness in which communication may be nonverbal. In such a relationship, the sexual act is certainly symbolic and expressive of this intimacy. When I discuss intimacy, I'm not referring to the game of mind reading. Rather, I'm suggesting that there can be sensitivity and awareness that go deeper than spoken words.

However, I believe that intimacy is also possible between relatives or friends. Corrie ten Boom and her sister, Betsie, reached this level.[1] I suspect that Paul and Timothy did also, as did David and Jonathan,

1. Corrie ten Boom, *The Hiding Place* (Old Tappan, NJ: Revell, 1974).

Mary and Elizabeth, Paul and Luke. And what about Jesus and John "the beloved disciple"?

Is not this the level at which God seeks eventually to relate to each of His children? What else could Paul have meant in 1 Corinthians 2:9–13, especially his reference to "the deep things of God"? At some point in our religious experiences, does not the indwelling presence of the Holy Spirit seek to bring about a relationship with God on this level? I believe so.

Intimacy is rare, and it takes time and commitment to develop it, but that is possible and worth the effort.

Consequences of Maintaining Superficial Relationships

There are certain consequences of going only partway in our relationships. That is, if we never progress to levels 6, 7, or 8 with anyone, then certain detrimental effects become obvious. I have observed that if a person never or rarely goes past level 5, the social-interaction level, with anyone, he will develop judgmental and critical attitudes and behavior. The person who tends to be critical of others, a faultfinder, and a negative sort of individual is generally one who has not reached the deeper levels of relating.

Judgmental attitudes and behavior are symptoms of a lonely person whose relationships tend to be superficial. A negative person often is one who has no close friends. Now which came first, the negativism or the absence of close relationships? That's hard to say categorically. Certainly this is a sort of vicious circle. Consequently, if you choose to avoid closeness, be prepared to pay a heavy price.

The reason why shallow relationships result in a judgmental lifestyle is simply that something essential for a healthy personality is missing: depth or closeness. A relational deficiency develops. God made us, as social creatures, to need meaningful relationships with others.

Just as our physical bodies suffer from a nutritional deficiency when we do not consume adequate amounts of vitamins, minerals, and various nutrients, so will our personalities suffer from a relational deficiency when we do not consume the support that comes from meaningful relationships. A hungry body will send out danger signals called hunger pains and eventually a neglected body will produce signs of illness and disease (dis-ease). Likewise, a deprived spirit will give out its danger signals: negative, critical, judgmental words and behavior. The person who complains a lot is telling us that he has a relational deficiency.

Consequences of Maintaining Close Relationships

There are also consequences of moving to the deeper levels of relating: caring, sharing, and intimacy with at least some people. These consequences are signs of a truly relationally healthy person.

People who develop some relationships on levels 6, 7, and 8 will in time automatically express nurturing attitudes and behavior. They will tend to avoid judging others and begin the beautiful process of nurturing others. They will soon recognize the futility of being critical of others' actions. Instead, they develop a new positive perspective with regard to persons.

This new perspective sees other humans not as isolated individuals striving for their own selfish goals but as potential familylike friends in need of each other, undergirding, supporting, sustaining, and affirming each other. This doesn't mean that there is never a time or place for criticism and judgment. What I am referring to is a general disposition: even when one is expressing judgment it will be done in a loving and affirming spirit and with a constructive goal in mind.

Even after judging and rebuking the Corinthian Christians, the apostle Paul could still say to them, "I am glad I can have complete confidence in you" (2 Cor. 7:16, NIV). He also reminded the Thessalonian believers that "we were gentle among you, like a nurse taking care of her children. So, being affectionately desirous of you, we were ready to share with you not only the gospel of God but also our own selves, because you had become very dear to us" (1 Thess. 2:7–8, RSV). Now that is nurture! Notice that the words *nurse* and *nurture* are related. Relating on the deeper levels will produce nurturing.

Relating on the deeper levels produces a nurturing spirit because a relational sufficiency exists. Mutual need-meeting takes place among people who nurture each other; this in turn produces interdependency and mutual support. Love at the deeper levels tends to reproduce itself. "We love because he first loved us" (1 John 4:19, NIV). If this is true between man and God, then it is equally true between man and man. Relational sufficiency fosters strong interpersonal relationships, just as nutritional sufficiency fosters strong bodies.

I have discovered that when my deeper relational needs are being met (via caring, sharing, and intimacy) an amazing strength becomes available and causes me to want to affirm those around me. This in turn results in a mutuality and reciprocity, which sets up a cycle of health and growth for all involved.

Some Probing Personal Questions

How deep are my relationships with others?

Do I recognize my basic human need for depth, closeness, and intimacy?

Am I hungry (i.e., motivated) enough to seek closer and deeper relationships? Am I willing to run the necessary risks?

Am I motivated enough to overcome my fear of intimacy? Am I willing to recognize not only that I need others but also that others need me?

Am I willing to work to remove the barriers to intimacy and closeness? Do I see the need for planning, structuring, and praying for opportunities for developing deeper relationships?

Am I willing to open myself to at least a few others around me in order to invite closeness? Am I willing to trust another to become a close and intimate friend?

2

You Go As Deep As You Trust

Achieving closeness with people, reaching the deeper levels of caring, sharing, and intimacy in one's relationships, requires faith—a trusting attitude toward others. My experience has taught me that you go as deep as you trust. Getting close to someone is possible only when you trust that person enough to allow him or her insight into your innermost self and when in return that person trusts you enough to allow you the same privilege. Trust is by its very nature personal, and if persons are going to relate meaningfully they have to trust each other. Trust is openness, and openness is the gateway to depth. Therefore, you go as deep as you trust.

The Trust Factor: A Priority

If you want to move from exclusively shallow relationships to deeper levels, then you have to make trust your first priority. However, seeking deeper relationships may be scary, so it will be crucial for you to believe that launching out into the deep is a significant need in your life. You need to make a sincere decision to try to fulfill this need.

It took me years to realize that deep relationships are important to my welfare and that of others around me. For many years I was a pastor preaching two to four times a week and fulfilling all my other pastoral duties. I had been brainwashed by my culture to believe that

33

pastors weren't supposed to get close to anyone. They were to have no "pets," no cliques, no close friends in the church. Treat everyone the same, we were told, which meant, practically speaking, keeping everyone at a safe distance. I was good at that. Even in high school, most people thought I was snobbish and distant. At least that's what my wife tells me (we attended the same high school).

For years even my sermons were distant: academic, intellectual, doctrinal, wordy, without vitality, bones without flesh and blood; docetic, dogmatized, and deodorized. Oh, I could shout, pound the pulpit, and use all the appropriate gestures of a traveling evangelist, but action and noise are not necessarily from the heart. I was the church's disc jockey with no music of my own. The tragedy was that that's the way I thought it should be. I was trained to be that way. The older preachers who were my models were that way.

I didn't have any close relationships. In those days, my wife and I were still trying to figure out each other and survive in an unstable marriage. I had "friends," and some people thought I was a nice fellow to be around. Every church I pastored grew under my leadership. But there were few truly close relationships with a depth of caring, sharing, and intimacy.

What brought about the change? A series of crises in my marriage, family, and career. Crisis has a way of exposing weak foundations, shoddy supports, and inadequate resources. I very slowly began to realize that I desperately needed the resources and support that could come only from some deep, meaningful, and personal relationships. This included a renewal of my relationship with God. It is very difficult for an ordained minister to admit this to himself, much less do anything about it. Yet, if I couldn't get squared away with God, how on earth could I develop any deep relationships with other people? I wasn't sure what to do, but I did recognize that I desperately needed some meaningful relationships.

I began reaching out to a few people my age who seemed to be looking for the same depth I was looking for. My wife, Carole, did the same thing. It was in a small prayer-and-share group that change began to occur, both with reference to God and to a few fellow pilgrims. It sounds extremely simple but it's true: when you reach out for deeper relationships, God not only will meet you but also will see to it that some others will be there (see Jer. 29:12–14; John 17:26).

Then I discovered that others needed me as much as I needed them. It was my wife who first taught me this. Carole was as hungry for depth and closeness as I was. Finding it together was the beginning of strengthening our marriage. As we reached out to a few people in our church, we found the same need in others. We all needed each other. Together we grew. Together we found depth.

Reaching the levels of caring, sharing, and intimacy requires commitment: taking the initiative, spending the time, running the risks of rejection, fumbling, and embarrassment, and making consistent efforts. Trust is commitment. Caring calls for commitment. Sharing your inmost feelings requires a sincere conviction that this is a primary means of developing depth in one's relationships. The deeper levels are not reached accidentally or incidentally but by design and determination. Developing close relationships may even call for sacrifice: giving up the routine of the trivial and going to the trouble of spending time and energy with fellow seekers in the quest for closeness.

Breaking with the Past

If I'm not careful, I will allow my past—mistakes, failures, misfortunes, sins, and disappointments—to muddle my present. W. Hugh Missildine once wrote a book entitled *Your Inner Child of the Past.*[1] That child keeps popping up in my life and causing all kinds of problems. I've learned now to tell that brat to get lost, go fly a kite, or go and bother somebody else. By learning to trust people in my closest relationships, I'm gradually breaking with my past.

My wife knows me well. She's taught me that I don't need to pretend to be somebody I'm not. I don't need to wear masks or to cover up the real me. We've taught each other how to trust the other with the knowledge of the real self. We've gradually learned to accept each other just as we are, warts and all.

When we married in 1952, Carole and I both thought the other was perfect. Naturally, I was more perfect than she! Our first serious argument took place about thirty days after the wedding. My Dulcinea turned into a witch. Her Prince Charming became a monster. Finally, after all the angry words, we sat crying on the floor of the bedroom closet! When you're twenty-one and nineteen and newly married, you don't need a reason for where you end up after a fight. But I'll never forget one of Carole's concluding statements as we were making up.

1. W. Hugh Missildine, *Your Inner Child of the Past* (New York: Simon and Schuster, 1963).

Through the tears came the words, "And I thought you were *perfect!*"
I always thought she had unususal perception. Anyhow, pretending
you're somebody you're not is a terrible way to live. The tension of
fearing you'll be found out will eat you alive.

When you trust your close friends, you stop the cover-up, take off
the mask, and allow your true self to come out. One of the amazing
things about doing that is that for most people the "real you" is a
nicer person to get to know and a much more likeable person than the
pretender.

Part of the past you break with as you learn to trust those close to
you is having lived with so many shallow relationships. So much of
our life has been consumed with living on levels 1–5 with most people.
Life is too short to waste so much of your life on those levels to the
almost total neglect of the deeper levels. Actually, I grew tired of the
shallows. So many of those relationships were phony and unproductive.

Learning to trust those around you moves you to break with the
past of exclusively shallow relationships. You continue to relate to
most of the people in your life on levels 1-5, but by going deeper you
find that you're not spending all of your time in relationships that go
nowhere. You still walk through the shallows every day but you no
longer waste all your precious moments there. You have experienced
the deeper levels.

However, one must first overcome fear of the deep. For example,
learning to swim was an ordeal for me. I was nearly twelve years old
before I really learned how. More than 80 percent of our community
swimming pool was five feet or less in depth, so I could maneuver over
a lot of water and still touch bottom. But I had never gone into that
20 percent at the north end of the pool where the diving boards were.
That end may as well have been 100 feet deep instead of 20 feet. I saw
it as the drowning end of the pool.

One day I decided that it was ridiculous for all of my peers—but
not me—to be able to swim. I don't know where I got the courage. I
really don't remember. I simply walked to the deep end of the pool,
jumped in, and swam for the rope and floats that separated the diving
area from the shallower area. You know, I made it! All of my fears
evaporated in the ecstasy of victory. I found out that if you want to do
something enough, you can do it. If others could swim, so could I. I
trusted my ability, the lifeguard (if anything went wrong), and the
water (to hold me up). My fear of the deep was gone. I had to keep
practicing, but learning to trust was the key to accomplishment.

A lot of people are afraid of deep relationships. This stems from fear of the unknown. It helps to know that friends are worth trusting. I don't know what else to say except, "Jump in." You'll never overcome fear of closeness until you take your "leap into the dark" with those few friends available to you. Trust them.

To launch out into deeper relationships requires courage. The word *courage* comes from the Latin *cor*, meaning "heart." To have courage is to have heart. Where does one find courage? I believe that God is an *en*-couraging God. He loves to put courage into people. To be encouraged is to have heart put into you. Have you ever heard yourself say, "I don't have the heart to do this"? God is in the business of putting a new heart into people (see Ezek. 36:26). Ask Him for the heart to launch out into deeper relationships.

There will be a surprise waiting for you: I discovered that in the deeper relationships is where Jesus is to be most often found. If you want to find Jesus, launch out into the deep. There are two significant passages in the Bible which suggest this.

The first is Isaiah 58:1–9. Read the passage carefully, noticing the descriptions of meaningful relationships with other people: the rebuking of shallow religious ritual (fasting) and the pretense of being religious but behaving cruelly (oppressing others, quarrelling, fighting); the need for humility, honesty, and caring for needy people; the importance of sharing food, house, and clothing with the destitute—in other words, getting involved in other people's lives at the point of their needs (level 6). The result?

> Then your light will break forth like the dawn,
>   and your healing will quickly appear;
> then your righteousness will go before you,
>   and the glory of the LORD will be your rear guard.
> Then will you call, and the LORD will answer;
>   you will cry for help, and he will say: Here am I.
>   [Isa. 58:8–9, NIV]

The second passage is Luke 24:13–35, the story of the appearance of the risen Jesus to the two disciples on the road to Emmaus. Luke records that these two depressed men, Cleopas and his unnamed friend, were met by Jesus as they traveled from Jerusalem to Emmaus shortly after Jesus' crucifixion. Their hopes and dreams had been shattered. Not recognizing Jesus, they engaged Him in conversation along the road, sharing their deep disillusionment over the death of their Master.

The sharing (level 7) experience must have been intense. Then verses 30–31 indicate that during the table fellowship that evening in their Emmaus home "their eyes were opened and they recognized him." Jesus revealed Himself in their deepest moments of sharing. Of course, this sort of experience is available only to Christians, true believers. Nonetheless, how many believers have yet to meet their Lord at these deeper levels of relating? Trust is the key as you break with the past and launch out into the deep of the present.

Cultivating Transparency

In recent years, psychologists have done considerable research about the cultivation of transparency; that is, self-disclosure to a few intimates.[2] There is great power and therapy in self-disclosure. In such meaningful experiences one finds greater self-knowledge and authenticity for living.

Exactly what is self-disclosure? It is telling another about yourself, honestly offering your thoughts and feelings (especially your emotions) for the other's reflection and evaluation, hoping that genuine open communication will follow. Becoming transparent means raising the shades and opening the windows of your innermost being to the awareness and understanding of another whom you trust and value.

The Power of Self-disclosure

One of my most recent serendipitous revelations concerned the power of self-disclosure. My wife and I first discovered this new power in one of our prayer-and-share small-group experiences. I learned that before I can fully know myself, it is necessary that a few significant other people know the deep aspects of my personality, especially my feelings. It became quite clear to me that to be distant from all other human beings is to be alienated from myself and to not know myself. Self-disclosure brought the power of self-knowledge.

Other people, the significant few who received my self-disclosure, became mirrors that reflected back to me my true self. Actually, all of us learned quite early to think much of what we perceived others thought of us. Charles Horton Cooley called this "the looking-glass

2. See Sidney M. Jourard, *The Transparent Self: Self-Disclosure and Well-Being*, 2d ed. (New York: Van Nostrand Reinhold, 1971) and *Self-Disclosure: An Experimental Analysis of the Transparent Self* (New York: Wiley, 1971; reprinted Melbourne, FL: Krieger, 1979).

self." The human self emerges or is fashioned in an ongoing process: how I imagine I appear to people whom I consider significant; how I imagine they judge and evaluate that appearance; and how I react to that perceived evaluation (some sort of emotional response, such as pride or mortification). I tend to imagine, and in imagining share, the evaluations of others concerning me.[3] As this process went on constantly over the several years of my early childhood, I grew to see myself as others saw me.

Significant others are still mirrors in which I see myself. As I open myself to others, they reflect back to me, both verbally and behaviorally, what they hear and see, along with such reactions as approval or disapproval. Their perceptions of the facts may be in error, but that doesn't matter. Whatever they perceive and reflect is what I will see about myself. It would be good if we would carefully select these significant others in our adult years so that we will receive as accurate a perception of ourselves as possible.

I also found that self-disclosure produces the power of attraction. Most people to whom I revealed myself were attracted to me. This is not easy to explain. Some fascinating research about attraction has been done and analyzed.[4] The dynamic involved here is reciprocity, the basic premise of which is: Self-disclosure begets self-disclosure. Related to this premise is another: Trust generates trust. Those I trust with my deepest confidences tend in return to trust me with theirs.

Researchers are giving us several valuable insights concerning self-disclosure: an exchange of intimate disclosures is necessary for the development of close relationships; some mutuality or reciprocity of the disclosure may be necessary for strong attraction to emerge; once a friendship is formed, routine reciprocation of disclosure is not necessarily needed or expected. Some research suggests that highly disclosing persons are better adjusted in their personalities than people who disclose less. The greater the likelihood of disclosure, the greater will be both marital and general satisfaction. For instance, the more a wife discloses, the more satisfied the husband will report himself to be, and vice versa.[5]

Moreover, it is not the amount of material disclosed that matters

3. Charles Horton Cooley, *Human Nature and the Social Order* (New York: Scribners, 1922), p. 184.
4. See Clyde Hendrick and Susan Hendrick, *Liking, Loving, and Relating* (Monterey, CA: Brooks/Cole, 1983), chapters 1–3. On self-disclosure and attraction, see pp. 42–45.
5. Ibid., pp. 198ff.

but the *type*: positive rather than negative. One can be *too* revealing. Total self-disclosure is a high-risk practice. No one needs or wants to hear all about another's sordid past, nor negative, critical, and judgmental feelings, nor complaints and nagging pessimisms. Satisfied married couples tend to disclose positive, important matters, while less happy couples talk about negative things of every level of importance. Being selective in disclosing one's feelings seems to be more beneficial to harmony in marriage than indiscriminate catharsis. What is disclosed should not be threatening information.

I also found how self-disclosure attracts when I preached confessional sermons.[6] When I showed the relevancy of the message in my personal life, people sat up and listened. Confessional preaching is not declaring all of the doubts, disbeliefs, and sins of your past or present. Rather, it is acknowledging to the congregation where you are in your own spiritual pilgrimage. Most church members naïvely believe that pastors have no problems living the Christian life, that every day is one long string of victories. They have a hard time identifying with such fictitious supermen.

Confessional preaching reveals the pastor as a real human being who does not necessarily find faith, prayer, love, integrity, and dedication easy or simple. People can identify with humanness. As a result of such preaching I found tremendous reciprocity and attraction from my people. "Hey, preacher, that's where I am. Maybe you have something to say after all!" Then there followed, "Preacher, let me tell you where I am. You seem to know what I'm struggling with." From then on, I never had an attendance problem.

Self-disclosure also can provide healing. Sharing your innermost feelings enables you to deal with them. Otherwise your emotions tend to control *you*. I've experienced a lot of stress in my life. Some stress is good for you. Too much can kill you.[7] When I can tell some confidants about the stressful factors in my life, I experience an amazing relief. These people can also offer some guidance on how better to deal with stress. Anger can be a devastating emotion when it is out of control. Disclosing the details of one's anger to an empathetic friend

6. John R. Claypool, *The Preaching Event* (Waco, TX: Word, 1980). However, I had begun doing this before I read Claypool's book.

7. See Hans Selye, *Stress Without Distress* (New York: Lippincott, 1974). Also, Ogden Tanner, *Human Behavior: Stress* (New York: Time-Life, 1976) and Keith W. Sehnert, *Stress/Unstress* (Minneapolis: Augsburg, 1981) provide excellent advice about how to cope with stress.

can result in wonderful healing. Fear can be paralyzing. To admit to being afraid can often bring needed assurances and renewed confidence.

Self-disclosure in the right context to Barnabas-type confidants brings the power of encouragement.[8] I have known several parents who, in prayer-and-share groups, have trusted confidants with stories about the burdens of rearing children who were runaways, drug abusers, dropouts from church, or something worse, and discovered unusual resources through the encouragement these close friends offered.

The Therapy of Honesty

As we think further about the trust factor (you go as deep as you trust), we realize that trust cultivates transparency by its insistence upon integrity in self-disclosure. Moreover, such honesty in self-disclosure produces a wonderful therapy.

First, as we reveal our inmost selves, there is a great release of burdens; that is, unresolved conflicts, unsettled resentments, nagging confusions, disturbing doubts. Everyone has his or her own bag of burdens. The release comes not in some magical resolving of the conflicts, settling of the resentments, clarifying of the confusions, answering of the doubts, and forgiveness of the wrongs by the simple verbalizing of these to others. No, the release comes in the beautiful fact that others now can help you bear the burdens. Burden-bearing at least halves the burdens. Paul advised bearing one another's burdens and so fulfilling the law of Christ, which is the law of love (Gal. 6:2). That's still good counsel.

This is difficult to explain, but burden-bearing in community (two or more) provides unusual healing. There is therapy in the honesty of self-disclosure, in the cultivation of transparency. Transparency brings light (the light of truth in—one hopes—the context of love) to the dark recesses of one's soul, and light has amazing healing powers.

Second, the therapy of honesty will be experienced in the fact that one's self-disclosure becomes an invitation to reciprocate. This opens a two-way channel of communication, a type of bibliotherapy, a therapy of honest words, telling it like it is, telling it like it feels. Then we discover that another person in this world is struggling with similar problems. However, more than this, the other person hears you, cares about you, and walks with you through the difficulty.

There is often an unusual attraction in reciprocity. This mutual

8. See Acts 4:36; 9:26–27; 15:36–41 for the story of Barnabas.

exchange of thoughts, feelings, and experiences results in mutual liking. It seems that having someone like us is a potent source of reward. Especially in American society there is a strong need to gain the approval and esteem of others. Consequently, perceiving that others like us has a powerful effect, even a healing effect.

Openness Allows Authenticity

When I am open with a close confidant, I feel myself to be more authentic and genuine. The *real* me is not always what shines on the outside, where I sometimes pretend to be someone I'm not. The real me is deep inside. When I allow myself to be transparent with another, I feel the real me showing through.

Furthermore, when I allow the real me to emerge I find that I am more open to change, a change for the better usually, which results in a *new* me. In addition, the real me and the new me, in the context of openness, result in a new *us* in the relationship. We are no longer just two people in occasional conversation. We become a pair: friends, confidants, fellow sharers. Notice how Paul the apostle referred to his cohorts (e.g., Rom. 16:7; 1 Cor. 3:9).

Authenticity is refreshingly freeing. Through my openness with others, I have discovered my own humanity. I am a human being. God made me such. I am "me," and that's okay. I don't have to be Mr. Perfect or Superman to be an authentic person. I make mistakes like anyone else. I have problems just like all humans do. It's acceptable to recognize myself as the imperfect yet genuine human that I am. I do not wear an *S* on my underclothes, and my wife doesn't wear a *W* (for Wonder Woman); we both wear an *H*. We're members of the human race, not some mythical super race. Such an awareness means freedom to be ourselves.

Risking Yourself to Others

When I trust you with the knowledge about who I am and what I am, I am risking myself to you. I trust you to accept me and anything I share with you. You could reject me, or make fun of me, or be confused about me, but I will trust you to hear, accept, and (I hope) understand me. It will be risky, but it will be the only way to develop a deep relationship between us.

When you risk yourself to others, you become vulnerable. The Latin root of "vulnerable," *vulnerare*, means "to wound." To become vulnerable means to be susceptible to injury, to be exposed to criticism; and this can hurt, especially if I am an insecure person.

However, I will very likely never learn much about myself nor develop an authentic relationship with you if I do not expose my innermost self to your knowledge and evaluation. New self-knowledge and a new and deeper relationship are at stake. Consequently, I can withhold myself from you and "play it safe" with my best mask on, or I can see the possibilities of an adventure: learning a great deal about myself and building a new relationship with you.

The more I have grown to accept my humanity, the more I've learned to value relationships over any form of pretense. When I trust you with knowledge of my true self, I am saying that our relationship is more important to me than giving you impressions about me that may not be genuine. If the truth about me is not an adequate foundation for a meaningful relationship, then we have no basis for a close relationship; trying to establish one is not worth my time or yours.

One very vital thing that makes trusting others much easier than it seems is that I have learned to trust God to develop the relationship. If God is in charge of my life (i.e., the sovereignty of God, a basic Christian belief), then when I share my feelings with others, I am also trusting God to use that openness to bring into existence whatever meaningful relationship the situation merits. If God is not working in the relationship, then it will be better for it not to develop.

Moreover, when I tell a confidant what I feel, and I am trusting God in the process, I find that God has an unusual ability to use that sharing to reveal something very important about myself to me. This is not what is commonly called introspection. It is revelation with the assistance of a caring and reflecting trustworthy friend.

However, a word of caution is necessary. Some matters out of a person's past ought not be shared or are not worth telling. Recalling some items from one's experiences could actually damage one's relationships. This is not a matter of a lack of trust; it is simply good common sense.

Wrongs that have been confessed to God and forgiven ought to be left alone and forgotten. Forgiven sins are buried in the forgetfulness of God, and we have no right to dig them up. The psalmist declared that a merciful and loving God removes our sins from us "as far as the east is from the west" (Ps. 103:12, NIV). That's quite a distance, I would say. A person who is forgiven by God is "clean" and washed "whiter than snow" (Ps. 51:7, NIV). Who are we to dirty things again by retelling sordid stories about wrongs that we settled long ago with our loving Father in heaven? In sharing, the emphasis should be on present feelings and not past deeds.

There are some rare exceptions, however, to this rule. If you are a former convict and you are about to propose marriage to a woman who doesn't know about your criminal record, then you should tell her. If she finds out later, which is likely, then she will feel betrayed and untrusted. A former marriage and divorce certainly ought to be made known to a future spouse. But if you've had one or more illicit sex relationships in the past and you've asked God's forgiveness, then let such matters stay in the dead past. However, if one of those relationships resulted in a child being born, then you should tell a future spouse. Have you had an abortion to terminate pregnancy out of wedlock? Claim God's offer of forgiveness and leave that wrong in the past covered by the mercy of God. Build for the future with the new opportunities God gives you in His grace. Learn from the past, but press on to the future. "Go, and sin no more" (John 8:11, KJV).

Finding Trustworthy People

To build close relationships you have to find some people who are worthy of your trust. This isn't always easy to do. Here are a few suggestions.

Not every person you may know qualifies to be trusted with knowledge about your innermost self. Some people don't want to know you intimately. They may decide that they don't have time for that close a relationship. They are satisfied with maintaining somewhat distant although pragmatic relationships. These people see you strictly in utilitarian terms. If you are useful to them in some practical way, then they will be friends, but never on any deep level.

Other people don't qualify because they can't be trusted to hold in confidence what you share. Still others don't qualify because they are easily frightened by closeness and depth. Sharing with these will simply overload their circuits.

You may have to use the trial-and-error method to find trustworthy people. It may seem that such people are rather rare.

As a Christian, I want to say that the place to begin looking for trustworthy people will be among the people of God. Of course, not all of them qualify, but they are more likely to. I'm talking about people who know and love God. They know something about trust, understanding, being sensitive to another's needs, listening and caring, the importance of being honest and authentic. These are the people who are more likely to understand the need for deep and meaningful relationships.

I'm not suggesting that you cannot have close relationships with non-Christians. However, as a Christian you will most probably find close friends among fellow Christians whose understanding of depth will be qualitatively different from that of people who do not and cannot understand the meaning of "the deep things of God" (1 Cor. 2:10, NIV). I realize that my experience is limited, but I've tried to relate on the deeper levels with non-Christians and none of them ever seemed to know what I was talking about.

It is encouraging to know that very often trustworthy people are looking for people like you and me and want to develop close rela- tionships. In my last pastorate, we started several small prayer-and- share groups, and in several instances people gravitated to our church because they had been looking for a small-group experience. When they heard by word of mouth about our groups, they were eager to join.

I believe that for every person like yourself who is looking for deep and meaningful relationships, God has some people looking for you to make the relationship possible. The people who are looking for you are the ones who will be trustworthy.

A good way to establish close relationships is to begin with only one or two people. Don't try to start with several. You will overload your own circuits if you do. Try sharing with just one person initially. If you're married, try your spouse. What better person could you start with? If you're single, look around for another single person, possibly someone you work with or someone you often see at church services and activities. Start by listening to those already nearest you. Listen- ing has amazing powers for opening up doors to deep relationships. By listening to another you will earn the right to share your innermost feelings. Reciprocation will take place and a close relationship will be born.

Levels of Trust

A person does not establish trust in a single or simple step. There actually are levels of trust. I have identified eight levels, which I will

now briefly list and explain. Try to decide if you are at any or several
of these levels as you evaluate your current closest relationships.

Level one: the distant level. I don't know anything about you, so I
will keep as great a distance from you as possible. I simply don't trust
you because you appear to me to be a mere stranger. Lack of knowledge, lack of trust.

Level two: the cautious level. What I know or see about you I like,
but I'm not sure I can trust you. Therefore, I will be cautious. I will
take my time and see if you are trustworthy, but I'm not going to rush
this.

Level three: the conditional level. What I know or see about you I
don't like, but I will try to change you into being someone I can like.
I will accept you, to some extent, but I have plans for your improvement.

Level four: the risk level. What I know about you I like, so I will try
to know you better. I will run some risks to trust you to get to know
me, too. At this point, the chances for developing a close relationship
look more positive than negative.

Level five: the hiding level. What I know about myself I don't like,
but I really want to do something about myself. I like what I see in
you, but I'm afraid that if you don't like what's in me, you'll reject me.
Therefore, I will try to hide from you as I try to get to know you.
Maybe I'll find out that you are the kind of person who will accept me,
warts and all. I hope so.

Level six: the sharing level. What I know about myself, I like. At least,
I like more things about me than I dislike. The things I dislike I accept.
Anyhow, I will try to share myself with you. I have some good things
about myself to share. I trust you to feel the same way.

Level seven: the mutual-acceptance level. I am tired of being alone,
disliking myself and others. I am going to take the risk of reaching out
to you, opening myself to you, allowing you to accept me as I try to
accept you. In our mutual acceptance maybe we will find something
new and enjoyable in each other as we relate. Maybe our relationship
can be that something new to accept, enjoy, and cultivate.

Level eight: the unconditional-acceptance level. I accept myself and
you unconditionally. I value you as a unique human being, loved by
God, created in God's image, someone for whom Christ died, a person
with some of the same needs I have, someone whom I can bless and
someone who can bless me. Together we can bless others about us.

Experiencing a New Self-image and Perception of Others

Understanding the concept of self-image is crucial to understanding human behavior. As persons see themselves, so will they behave. A poor or negative self-image usually causes one to behave in uncooperative, critical, judgmental, or even destructive ways. If I see myself as "no good," then I will more likely behave in ways that cause others to evaluate me as "no good." If I see myself as "stupid," then I will set out to prove it by my behavior. On the other hand, a good, positive self-image will produce relatively meaningful, productive, altruistic behavior.

Developing deep and close relationships wherein I am accepted unconditionally and can share my innermost feelings brings about a more positive and warmly accepting self-image. As another accepts and loves me with care and understanding, I am more likely to accept and love myself. A more positive self-image results from this.

As my self-image improves, so does my perception of others. I am less likely to see the faults of others and instead see the potential for good in their lives. This in turn encourages others to behave accordingly. All of us usually behave in such a way as to fulfill the expectations of the significant others in our lives.

What is the true source of my new self-image and perception of others? As a Christian and a person made in the image of God, I recognize that newness is a special gift from God. "Therefore, if anyone is in Christ, he is a new creation; the old has gone, the new has come!" (2 Cor. 5:17, NIV). My new self-image is a *given*, not something to be earned by performance. I have a new self-image "which is being renewed in knowledge in the image of its Creator" (Col. 3:10, NIV). Trusting and loving relationships assist me in experiencing what is already mine from God.

Striking It Rich

In recent years old oil and gas wells in parts of Oklahoma and Texas have begun to produce again. Those old wells extended five to ten thousand feet underground and then played out. But with increased prices for gas and oil providing additional incentive and with better drilling equipment, oil-field drillers have now gone to levels around thirty thousand feet deep and have again struck it rich. There's a lot more black gold and gas at the deeper levels.

This is also true in interpersonal relationships. If you never go past level 5 (the social-interaction level) with anyone, you'll soon play out. Relational deficiency will set in and you'll become a judgmental, critical, hard-to-get-along-with person. We all need to go on to the deeper levels to strike it rich in our relationships with others and develop into a nurturing, affirming, caring, and sharing person. That is what this book is all about. In the chapters ahead I will carefully examine each level and offer suggestions about how to keep moving toward the deeper levels.

3

Why You and I Avoid People

Level 1 in our relationships has been identified as the avoidance level, which is the shallowest level of all. There are two types of avoidance, one positive, the other negative. If people are so important in our lives, then why do you and I avoid certain people? Here are some of the reasons I have discovered.

Necessary Avoidance

The positive type of avoidance is necessary. There is no way we can meaningfully relate to everyone. There are certain expected limitations placed upon most relationships.

First of all, I simply do not have the time to speak to everyone I see, much less relate on a meaningful level. There are only so many hours and minutes in the day. If I stopped to speak to everyone I see, I would never get where I am going. Most of the time my job and other objectives make me keep walking down the street or the hall.

Most of us are very busy people. We operate on the basis of schedules, appointments, the clock. Our responsibilities keep us moving on past most people. Moreover, especially in today's urban society, there are simply too many people to relate to in any meaningful way. Our crowded world makes relationships difficult to develop. Most people, it seems, have to be passed by or avoided.

For example, on the campus where I teach we have more than four thousand students and school personnel; we used to have only seventeen hundred in the 1950s. We are overwhelmed with students. Ours is the largest graduate theological school in the world, even in the history of Christendom. Our classes are large, too large. We just try to do the best we can. I have found it very difficult to learn the names of all my students, much less get to know them on a meaningful level. I get to know a few meaningfully but not many. We're all simply too busy. It isn't a great deal different pastoring a large church or working for a corporation. This is the nature of our urban society.

In addition, there are times when I am so involved in my work, so preoccupied with what I'm doing that I simply overlook most people who come into my sphere of awareness. My mind is on something else. It rarely occurs to me to speak to everyone or stop and converse. You could call this mere oversight or unintentional avoidance. The truth of the matter is that a lot of the other people around me are preoccupied also.

Finally, there are some days when I have deadlines to meet, projects to complete, quotas to fill, letters to write, phone calls to make, lectures to prepare, and books to read. Then I simply have to decide which comes first: work or people.

A former colleague of mine was totally a people person. When anyone dropped into his office, he would set everything else aside and give that person his full attention. Most of the time he never got much else done. His lectures were often unfinished. He never published. He rarely finished reading a book. For him, a teacher, teaching took second place to people.

Most teachers I know aren't that extreme. They try to be good teachers, which requires a lot of disciplined hard work. Their priorities are such that they cannot do everything. So they avoid a lot of people. They lock their office doors or go to the library. It is necessary to avoid most people in your life most of the time if you're going to get your work done. This means you make room for only a few in your circle of friends.

Intentional Avoidance

The negative type of avoidance is intentional, what I call the fine art of snubbing. These ignored people are the ones we simply do not like and wish to have little or nothing to do with. There are several reasons why we intentionally avoid certain people. These reasons may say as much about us as they do about the people we avoid.

Sometimes we avoid people because of a previous negative experience. When I was in grade school, a bully pushed me off my bicycle one day. He was too big to push back, so I simply avoided him from then on. As a pastor I've had church members who were very critical of me. I tended to avoid such people if I had the chance. Today I have some students who whine a lot over just about anything expected of them, and others who want to tell me all the details of their life story. I tend to avoid these if I can. Of course, those who have serious problems find that I will counsel with them as long as they need me.

In one of my pastorates we had a woman who was a hypochondriac. Every time I asked her how she was feeling, she would launch into a long and detailed explanation of her health problems. She seemed to enjoy telling it. I didn't enjoy listening, so I soon learned not to ask her how she felt. Before long, I was intentionally avoiding her.

At other times, we prejudge people. There are some people whom I have prejudged as people I didn't like. There was no specific reason. Probably it was due to something about their looks. When we once moved to a new church, my wife told me that, after one conversation, she had already decided that she wasn't going to like one of the ladies in the congregation. Why? "I don't know; there's just something about her I don't like." Within a few months, they became the best of friends, but at first an unexplainable prejudice caused Carole to avoid this woman. The way a person talks, dresses, behaves, or appears simply triggers something inside us that causes us to avoid that person.

A few times in my life I have grown a beard. Each time I discover that there are people who automatically classify a man with a beard as undesirable, a liberal, a hippie, or some other negative type. This happened in one of my pastorates. After I shaved my beard, one of our elderly members, a lady who had no idea what she was really saying, saw me in church the next Sunday and commented with delight, "Oh, we've got our preacher back!" For her, preachers and beards were incompatible. My beard had destroyed her preacher. Shaving got him back. What logic! I long to tell such narrow-minded people: "The beard is God's idea; shaving is man's idea." Probably all of the heroes of the Bible (including Jesus) wore beards. However, prejudice does not listen to reason. Incidentally, thanks to scholar-author Francis Schaeffer, beards and long hair are becoming the hallmarks of a conservative Christian! I believe that God is distressed over our allowing such trivia to disrupt relationships with people.

Furthermore, we avoid some people because we are afraid of them. I'm not referring to truly dangerous people, although we naturally avoid them too. I am thinking of people we perceive as smarter than we are or people who, because of their higher social standing and greater wealth, make us feel uncomfortable. Such people may intimidate us. We are overawed by them, so we avoid them.

These feelings are probably rooted in one's sense of insecurity. I have a theory that arrogant people tend to be very insecure. These overbearing and presumptuous people are actually afraid of others and are expressing their own deep insecurity. A well-known religious figure in the Bible Belt appears quite pompous in most of his photographs for publicity and carefully avoids any association with other religious leaders if he believes they are tainted with any form of theological liberalism. The man's unfriendliness toward the "liberals" is actually a symptom of his own insecurity. This reminds me of a sermon outline a preacher had prepared. In the margin beside his third point, he had written, "Weak point, shout here." A lot of the noise some arrogant folks make is really a cover-up for insecurity.

We avoid still other people because we deeply resent something they once said or did. This resentment springs from a previous negative experience but goes much deeper to become anger. I know of a church where two families had avoided each other for years. One family sat on one side of the auditorium and the other on the opposite side. They spoke to each other only if absolutely necessary. The resentment between them went back several years to an incident involving a deep disagreement over the calling of a pastor. Unkind words escalated into deep resentments. The other members of the church had long forgotten the incident, but these two families were still not speaking or having anything to do with each other. Needless to say, their behavior and attitudes were a disgrace to the church. There are some people like this in almost every church and community. Fortunately, most Christians are not this way.

This type of avoidance reflects emotional immaturity. The evasion is an effort to avoid confrontation and an unwillingness to seek reconciliation and forgiveness. This sort of thing can happen in a marriage. We usually call it pouting, something children are sometimes known for doing! This spoiled "inner child of the past" has a way of popping up under stress or difficulty and dominating an adult's behavior and attitudes.

Some people may "deserve" to be avoided! Does this sound too harsh and unchristian? Some people are downright obnoxious. It seems that everything about them is offensive. (The Latin word *obnoxiosus*, from which "obnoxious" comes, means "injurious.") Some people exhibit terrible personal habits and vulgar behavior and use profane language. The attitudes and behavior of some people are thoroughly repulsive and disgusting.

I am not suggesting that Christians should altogether avoid such people. These people are this way externally because they are this way internally. They need the moral and spiritual transformation of the gospel of Jesus Christ, and only Christians can or will bring that good news to them. I am only saying that the way some people behave is the reason they are avoided by decent and respectable people, Christian or not.

Some people are avoided because they are irritating. There are the constant talkers who never listen. There are the loud and boisterous. We once had some neighbors behind our back yard who often opened all their windows and played rock music so loudly that the sound reverberated throughout the entire neighborhood. Several neighbors asked them if they would turn down the volume of their stereo. They simply replied, "We like it that way." Only a call to the police to enforce the town's noise ordinance would produce results, temporarily. These people had no friends in the neighborhood, obviously.

In much the same way, smokers are irritating to nonsmokers. Few smokers seem to realize that their smoke is offensive to most nonsmokers. Even when they are told it is, they usually act offended themselves. Their persistence, of course, is due more to their drug addiction (nicotine) than any other reason. Many nonsmokers are actually allergic to tobacco smoke and can be made ill by breathing it. Many, although not all, smokers do not care when they are told this. "This is a free country, isn't it? I'll do as I please." With all the evidence available about the link between smoking and lung cancer, heart trouble, emphysema, and other diseases, you'd think that smokers would get rid of this dangerous and offensive habit. But these folks are victims of a drug addiction. So they will be avoided by many people who can't tolerate the smoke.

The Bible Speaks about People to Avoid

It's amazing how the Bible speaks about the subject of certain people to be avoided by Christians. Notice, however, that it's not the people as such but their behavior that is the important thing. Their behavior reflects certain values that are contrary to the Christian faith and life. A brief survey of the Gospel of Matthew, some of Paul's letters, and the general Epistles is revealing.

In Matthew's Gospel, the church was instructed to avoid certain people: those who reject the Christian message and messengers ("If anyone will not welcome you or listen to your words, shake the dust off your feet when you leave that home or town," 10:14, NIV); those who ridicule the Christian faith ("Do not give dogs what is sacred; do not throw your pearls to pigs. If you do, they may trample them under their feet, and then turn and tear you to pieces," 7:6, NIV); those who teach doctrinal error, manifested in their unethical behavior ("Watch out for false prophets. . . . By their [evil] fruit you will recognize them," 7:15–16, NIV); those who are dangerous (e.g., Herod, 2:13); those who are religious hypocrites (e.g., Pharisees, who were insensitive, unbelieving, and hardhearted, 12:14–15, 24–37; 13:10–15, 53–58; 15:13–14; 16:5–12); those who are stumbling blocks to young Christians (18:6ff.); the stubbornly unrepentant, who refuse to listen to the church's appeals (18:15–17); the callously unforgiving (18:21–35); the rigidly legalistic, who have no feelings of compassion for those in need (23).

Paul also instructed his churches to avoid certain kinds of people: those who create dissensions over doctrinal matters (Rom. 16:17; cf. 1 Cor. 1:10–17; 11:17–19); those who are blatantly immoral, who engage in incestuous relations and in relations with prostitutes (1 Cor. 5; 6:9–11, 15–20); those who engage in idolatry (1 Cor. 10:6–14); those extremists who cause confusion in worship (1 Cor. 14, especially v. 38); those whose behavior makes for "bad company" (1 Cor. 15:33, NIV); those who refuse to love the Lord (1 Cor. 16:22).

Moreover, Christians are to avoid an overly close relationship with unbelievers (1 Cor. 6:14–7:1); those leaders who are arrogant and deceitful (2 Cor. 11:13–15); those who live sensually and in disobedience to the Word of God (Eph. 5:5–14; Phil. 3:2ff., 17–19); those whose lifestyle is characterized as "evil" (Rom. 12:9; 1 Thess. 5:22); those who refuse to obey the teachings of Scripture (2 Thess. 3:14–15); those who stir up controversies and quarrels (2 Tim. 2:23; Titus 3:9); those who parade godless chatter or speculation as if it were the truth (1 Tim. 6:20–21; 2 Tim. 2:16); those who are "lovers of themselves, lovers of money, boastful, proud, abusive, disobedient to their parents, ungrateful, unholy, without love, unforgiving, slanderous, without self-control, brutal, not lovers of the good, treacherous, rash, conceited, lovers of pleasure rather than lovers of God—having a form of godliness but denying its power. Have nothing to do with them" (2 Tim. 3:2–5, NIV).

In the general Epistles of 2 Peter, 3 John, and Jude, similar references distinguish certain types of people Christians should avoid: false teachers who are identified largely by their immoral and unethical behavior rather than merely false ideas (2 Peter 2:1–22); arrogant leaders (3 John 9–11); troublemakers known for their unethical behavior as well as false teachings (Jude 4–16, 18–19). It is possible for one to be very orthodox or conservative in theology (by what one "says") and yet be very unethical in behavior. That's why the New Testament teaches that the real measure of a person's orthodoxy is not what one says but what one does (Matt. 25:31–46). Orthodoxy without orthopraxy is veiled heresy.

Preventing Self-righteous Avoidance

It may seem that the early Christians were advised to withdraw from the world and avoid all contact with non-Christians. Not so. Avoidance was recommended primarily in dealing with people whose behavior was extreme: the stubborn, the arrogant, the bullheadedly immoral. Christians need to be careful that their avoidance of certain kinds of people does not become a self-righteous avoidance.

Christians are to be "in" but not "of" the world. The New Testament writers were thoroughly committed to the teaching of Jesus that His disciples were to be *in* the world as witnesses of His life and love but not *of* the world and participating in its manner of living and thinking (John 17:6–19). Paul certainly did not avoid contact with the world. No ascetic monk in retreat was he.

In commenting upon 2 Corinthians 6:14–18 ("Be ye not unequally yoked together with unbelievers . . . ," KJV), Philip Edgcumbe Hughes says,

> It would be a serious mistake to conclude that Paul is here condemning all contact and intercourse with non-Christians: isolationism of this sort would, as he has previously written (1 Cor. 5:10), logically necessitate departure from the world. In other words, it is a position of absurdity. The pharisaical attitude of exclusiveness was discarded by him once for all at his conversion, and his whole ministry and manner of life was a denial of any policy of total withdrawal for fear of contamination from unbelievers. He, if anyone did, sought unremittingly to fulfil our Lord's commission to go *into all the world* and preach the gospel *to every creature.*

Furthermore, Paul

> made it his practice to conform to the pattern of the society in which he
> found himself, without, however, in any way compromising the integrity
> of the faith or lowering the high standards of Christian morality, and all
> with the great objective of winning others for Christ.

It was Paul who had said, "I have become all things to all men so that
by all possible means I might save some" (1 Cor. 9:22, NIV). Therefore,
Hughes continues,

> it may be that some of the Corinthian Christians had misinterpreted and
> misused these words of the Apostle as an excuse for entering into unholy
> alliances with unbelievers. The metaphor of the yoke which he uses
> here (2 Cor. 6:14) shows that he is thinking of close relationships in
> which, unless both parties are true believers, Christian harmony cannot
> be expected to flourish and Christian consistency cannot fail to be
> compromised.[1]

Christians are not to be isolated but insulated from the world. We
are not to retreat but to entreat.

In one community where I once lived, I tried three times to have
lunch with a fellow pastor who identified himself as a fundamentalist
Presbyterian and an avid disciple of Francis Schaeffer. He always had
an excuse, and so I stopped calling. He never called me. He thought
all Southern Baptists were liberals. He refused to have anything to do
with anything worldly: civic clubs, movies, state colleges, and Southern Baptist preachers! He maintained a thoroughly aloof stance. This
was not the strategy of Jesus and His disciples, nor is it the approach
of most conservative Presbyterians.

Moreover, the unchurched need us. My reading of the New Testament about what Jesus did and what the early Christians did convinces me that the unchurched people in our communities need our
witness, friendship, and acceptance as persons. If Christians have anything to offer non-Christians, then they ought to give it to them, not
run and hide.

Most unchurched people I have gotten to know are not like those
types the New Testament warns Christians to avoid. They are people

---

1. Philip Edgcumbe Hughes, *Paul's Second Epistle to the Corinthians*, New International Commentary on the New Testament series (Grand Rapids: Eerdmans, 1962),
pp. 245–46. Italics his.

who simply have never read much of the Bible, have rarely been invited to attend a church, have never been confronted with a simple and clear presentation of the gospel of Jesus Christ, and are waiting for folks like me to reach out to them with God's kind of love and acceptance.

To prevent self-righteousness and a holier-than-thou attitude, I have found it important to balance avoidance with penetration. This was Jesus' strategy: constant contact with all kinds of people, religious and irreligious, morally upright and flagrantly immoral, healthy folk and the sick, the politically strong and the powerless. He retreated with his disciples for teaching, prayer, and meditation where it was quiet and where they could be alone, yet later interacted directly with large numbers of people with all sorts of problems and difficulties. Each of the Gospel accounts highlights this blend of withdrawal and penetration, retreat and ministry, avoidance and involvement.

The apostle Paul followed the same strategy. He ventured directly into the marketplace or the courts of political power, yet avoided becoming "one of them." He balanced separation with engagement. One of the many interesting passages that illustrates this is Paul's advice in 1 Corinthians 10:23–11:1 (NIV).

"Everything is permissible"—but not everything is beneficial. "Everything is permissible"—but not everything is constructive. Nobody should seek his own good, but the good of others.

Eat anything sold in the meat market without raising questions of conscience, for, "The earth is the Lord's, and everything in it."

If some unbeliever invites you to a meal and you want to go, eat whatever is put before you without raising questions of conscience. But if anyone says to you, "This has been offered in sacrifice," then do not eat it, both for the sake of the man who told you and for conscience' sake—the other man's conscience, I mean, not yours. For why should my freedom be judged by another's conscience? If I take part in the meal with thankfulness, why am I denounced because of something I thank God for?

So whether you eat or drink or whatever you do, do it all for the glory of God. Do not cause anyone to stumble, whether Jews, Greeks or the church of God—even as I try to please everybody in every way. For I am not seeking my own good but the good of many, so that they may be saved. Follow my example, as I follow the example of Christ.

Notice that Paul saw no basic problem with a Christian buying meat in a pagan marketplace or eating a meal in an idol-worshiper's home. If the meat had been offered on the altar of a pagan god, then one ought not eat it for the sake of others' consciences. There is no point in giving offense or in compromising one's beliefs. By considering the facts of each situation, a Christian ought to be able to balance avoidance ("flee from idolatry," 1 Cor. 10:14, NIV) and penetration ("go, eat whatever is put before you," 1 Cor. 10:27, NIV).

Moreover, total avoidance or withdrawal means loss of the opportunity for witness. I exist in this world for the benefit of others. "Nobody should seek his own good, but the good of others" (1 Cor. 10:24, NIV). If I avoid everyone I don't like or approve of, then how will I ever be able to be a blessing to them? There are some people with whom I would just as soon not associate. But they need me, a Christian. And, in one sense, I need them. Strange as it may seem, I may be obnoxious to the obnoxious! After all, the so-called obnoxious are probably that way because they "ain't been hugged in over twenty-five years." A part of God's mission for me is to love them. I can't do that if I totally withdraw from them.

Preventing Intentional Avoidance

How can one prevent the negative (i.e., intentional) kind of avoidance? Here are some suggestions.

Reevaluate the past. Those previous negative experiences can be reevaluated. Reevaluation may call for new information. A man once criticized me considerably for my pastoral leadership. It seemed he disliked everything I did and said so publicly every chance he got. Consequently, I avoided him whenever possible. The situation, however, worsened. So I decided to find out what was really bothering him. I invited him out to lunch. I went to his home. I asked about his job, his family, and his feelings about life. I talked with some of his closest friends about him.

Here's what I learned. Some of his criticisms were valid and I sought to correct some of my ways of doing things. He had experienced three failures in a row in his business career; his wife was facing surgery for a brain tumor that could prove to be fatal; he didn't believe anyone at the church, except his wife and children, really cared about him. My whole perspective of this man changed. He didn't need my avoidance; he needed me to care about him and his situation.

If you can learn "where people are coming from," it can make a great deal of difference in how you respond to them. With few exceptions, the people who have given me the hardest time in my life have been people who were undergoing extreme difficulties in their own personal lives, and I was unaware of it at the time.

You can also try to discover why you dislike certain people. Talk with a close friend about your dislike of these people you avoid. Such a friend may be able to help you to see the reasons for your dislikes. Maybe a person you dislike is really loud and boisterous, or his or her smoking irritates your allergies, or his or her values are contrary to yours, or his or her intelligence makes you feel inferior and is intimidating. It helps to at least *know* what the bothersome factor is.

Once you identify what these reasons for disliking are, then you are better prepared to decide what is really important: your dislikes or that person's welfare? Only you can decide, but talking with a close friend can help.

If you are afraid of certain people you avoid, you can take charge of your feelings and face up to the nature and reality or unreality of these fears. Where the other person is superior to you in one sense, you are probably superior to him or her in another sense. Everybody can be an expert in something. Most of our fears of other people are unfounded and unnecessary. "There is no fear in love. But perfect [mature] love drives out fear" (1 John 4:18, NIV).

The anger we nourish toward some people can be resolved. If you avoid a person because of something he or she said or did in the past, recognize that your resentment is nothing more than cherished anger, which in the long run harms you more than the other person. Anger can be a powerful emotion, either to move you to change something or to move you to seek revenge.

Avoiding a person you resent is an effort to punish that person. The truth is that none of us is very good at punishing another, and by trying to do so we really hurt ourselves more than anyone else. Anger can be resolved in a very simple way (I didn't say easy—I said simple): through forgiveness. It is within your power to do this. Whatever it was that offended you can be forgiven by you.

Paul's formula was: "Get rid of all bitterness, rage and anger, brawling and slander, along with every form of malice. Be kind and compassionate to one another, forgiving each other, just as in Christ God forgave you" (Eph. 4:31–32, NIV). If you are a Christian, then there is the answer. As God forgave you: through Christ's death on the cross on your behalf for your sins, unconditionally, sacrificially, redemptively, and purposefully. If you are not a Christian, then you have

another prior problem and that is the need to experience God's for-
giveness for yourself through a personal commitment of your life to
Jesus Christ. Let me ask you, is the anger really worth hanging onto?
There is a solution.

Sometimes one's relationship with another is such that the best
way to resolve a complex difficulty is to discover the value of constructive and loving confrontation. This doesn't always work; it requires
cooperation and the other person may not want to resolve the difficulty between you. I have found that going directly to an antagonist
of mine (whom I would rather simply avoid) and asking for his or her
understanding and cooperation in resolving our differences while honestly admitting my own faults in the matter is often the best way to
rebuild a friendship. One is more likely to resolve differences by admitting one's own faults, asking for reconciliation, burying the past,
and building a friendship for the future rather than by being critical,
defensive, and accusatory.

Most people we avoid don't think we really love them, which is
probably true. There are some people I cannot love in my own strength
or will. However, maybe I can let Christ love these people through
me: the obnoxious, the repulsive, the disgusting. Maybe they are that
way largely because no one has ever really accepted and loved them
unconditionally. "Ain't nobody hugged me in over twenty-five years."
And one hug turned a killer into a Christian. The power of a hug is
often the power of love.

4

Hello, How Are You?

You can always tell when you're in west Texas because when you're driving down a country road or a cross-county highway and you meet another vehicle, everybody waves. It's the same way in my hometown of Frederick, Oklahoma, in the southwestern part of the state. As you walk down the sidewalk, everybody says, "Howdy," or "Hi there," or "Hello, how are you?" This is level 2: the greeting level.

Being Friendly

Being friendly is an important part of the human experience. Most people, going anywhere and doing anything, look for a friend. It sure beats being alone. No one likes to be alone for long, even in a crowd. Greeting people is a kind of a search for a friend.

It can be a lonely world. Even when he is surrounded by a large number of people, a person can feel very lonely and ignored. On our honeymoon, my wife and I visited a very large church in downtown Denver. There were several hundred people present. We arrived early for morning worship and after the benediction did not rush away. Yet not one person spoke to us. We were totally ignored. What a difference there would have been in our attitude toward worship that morning if some of the people, even an usher, had spoken a friendly "hello" to us. Being a young Baptist minister with his new bride, I thought we deserved better than that in a Baptist church!

As I'm writing this, I am in my second term as a visiting scholar
with Regent's Park College of Oxford University. On Sundays, I often
visit St. Aldates (Anglican) Church in Oxford. It is a very warm
evangelical church led by a loving and deeply dedicated rector, Canon
Michael Green. His spirit is contagious and has developed an actively
friendly congregation. Although I'm a total stranger from America,
these people always reach out in the warmest of friendship. After almost two hours of worship, few are in a hurry to leave. Their friendship
is meaningful and deep. That means a great deal to one who is a long
way from home and all alone. Alone but not alone!

It can be a lonely world in a booming urban society. As the popu-
lation grows our suicide rate increases. It is sad for so many to take
their own lives while being surrounded by many potential friends.
Drug abuse is epidemic in our urban centers. These are lonely people
who cannot tolerate their loneliness in the midst of all these others.
So many of us are "the lonely crowd."

As a pastor I discovered a large number of marriages that were
basically lonely relationships. The initial love had cooled; the children
for the wife and the job for the husband had become all-consuming
interests. As a couple they had lost touch with each other even while
sleeping in the same bed night after night.

We need each other, we really do. The theme of this book is that we
need each other. I don't care who you are or what your background
is. You need a friend, someone you consider an acquaintance who
knows and recognizes you. That friend needs you in the same way. A
true friend is something money cannot buy. If money brought you
together, then probably you aren't truly friends.

Recognizing someone you know in a crowded downtown area of a
large city when you thought you were all alone amidst strangers is an
exhilarating experience with which we are all familiar. It illustrates
the value we place on someone who knows, recognizes, and greets us.
There is a little extra bit of pleasure in being warmly greeted by a
friend. It's even a good feeling to be warmly greeted by someone you
hardly know. I believe that subconsciously all of us desire to be greeted
and thus recognized. Even on this level, we need each other.

When I greet someone, I am not only acknowledging his or her
presence; I am also, to some degree, saying, "I want to know you." I
am reaching out to that person. I am also hoping that person will
reciprocate and reach out to me. Greeting is that initial step in getting
to know someone.

Greeting is also a hope in the form of a question: "Do you want to know me?" I hope you do. Regardless of what I think of myself, I hope you will think enough of me to return my greeting. Have you ever had the experience of greeting someone with a cheery "hello" and getting nothing but a blank stare, as though you didn't exist? That leaves a very empty feeling. Immediately you ask yourself "What did I do, or say?" or "What's wrong with her?" My greeting is an invitation for you to get to know me. Most greetings aren't that serious, but at least the potential is there.

A friendship has to be started in some way by some one. The greeting gives us that chance. We'll never know each other if we don't try. A few days ago I met a physician from Ireland over morning tea. This morning on my way to the library we met on St. Giles Avenue and spoke as we recognized each other. I think a friendship is on the way. A small matter this is, but a building requires many small bricks. A greeting can be a meaningless gesture; it all depends upon what two people put into it and what they do to further a relationship. The problem in our urban society is that so often we neglect the greeting altogether.

Churches are learning a lot about the value of greeting. One church I served calls its ushers "greeters." Upon greeting a visitor, the greeter takes the guest to a register book in the foyer so the visitor's name and address can be recorded. It's a kind of ceremony saying, "You are significant and we want to know you." These names are then given to the pastor during the service so that after the benediction he can more accurately welcome these people at a special reception for guests in the church parlor. It's a memorable occasion when many friendships are begun. This is so much more than politely ushering a visitor to a seat. It's an *event* where strangers are invited to become friends.

How many times have you heard someone say, "I went to that church last Sunday but no one spoke to me; I'm not going back"? I felt this way about the church in Denver. Had we just moved to Denver, I doubt if we'd have ever gone back to that church. However, friendship is a two-way street. The number of people we confronted that morning was fewer than a dozen. If I had known the particulars about each one of them that day, maybe I would have had a different attitude. What if one was not feeling well, another had buried her mother the previous week, another had gone through a divorce, another had just lost his job, and the others were out-of-town visitors themselves! You never know what's going on in other people's hearts.

A family in one of my pastorates moved to a university town for one year so that the father-husband could do some graduate work. The first four Sundays in their new location they attended a local church. No one spoke to them. But that didn't stop this gregarious family. They began reaching out to the local members as if their roles had been reversed. Before long new friendships developed. They joined all the church organizations that were geared to their interests or ages and blessed that church for the year they were there. Incidentally, that church had been through some very difficult days with its then-current pastor and his entire staff. This experience had left the membership generally demoralized. Their unfriendliness was actually a mix of discouragement, depression, and confusion. It pays not to criticize someone until you've walked in his or her shoes.

Biblical Greetings

It was a common Jewish custom in biblical times to greet another with the salutation of peace. One account of Jesus' resurrection appearances contains two identical greetings for His disciples: "Peace be with you" (John 20:19, 21, NIV). The angel Gabriel greeted Mary with news of her future: "Hail, O favored one, the Lord is with you!" (Luke 1:28, RSV). Sometimes a greeting is simply mentioned: "At that time Mary . . . greeted Elizabeth" (Luke 1:39–40, NIV).

Paul's letters contain many greetings or encouragements to greet one another. "Grace and peace to you" was Paul's common method of greeting a church in a letter (e.g., Rom. 1:7; 1 Cor. 1:3; 2 Cor. 1:2; Gal. 1:3, NIV). His greetings to Timothy read, "Grace, mercy and peace" (1 Tim. 1:2; 2 Tim. 1:2, NIV). All of his letters begin with some such greeting that reflects the grace and peace of God discovered in the believer's relationship with Jesus Christ.

Paul also urged believers to greet one another or specifically named people on his behalf. One chapter in Romans contains several requests for greetings to be passed on (Rom. 16:3–16). Paul would sometimes urge his fellow Christians to "greet one another with a holy kiss" (Rom. 16:16; 1 Cor. 16:20; 2 Cor. 13:12; 1 Thess. 5:26, NIV). Philippians ends with a great crescendo of greetings: "Greet all the saints in Christ Jesus. The brothers who are with me send greetings. All the saints send you greetings, especially those who belong to Caesar's household" (Phil. 4:21–22, NIV). Aquila and Prisca and their church sent "hearty greetings" (1 Cor. 16:19, RSV). The early Christians knew how to greet one another in joy, love, and excitement. Churches today would do well to recover this lost art of Christian greeting.

Acknowledging One Another

What is a greeting but an acknowledging of one another? To acknowledge persons is to own to knowing them, to take notice of them, to recognize their presence and status. Acknowledgment can be a form of acceptance.

Greeting is truly a universal language. It is a form of acceptance. Some anthropologists believe that the wave of or extending of the hand goes back to the primitive practice of revealing to others that one had no weapons in hand. One was being greeted in peace. *Shalom* (peace) is a verbal expression of this among Jews, while *salam* is the same expression among Arabs. Whatever the manner or language, the greeting is universal: good morning, *guten Morgen, bon jour, buenos días,* aloha, *shalom,* or *salam.* Such is the search for or acknowledging of a friend.

We have already noted that Paul nearly always began his letters with the word *grace.* The term implies unconditioned acceptance. God accepts us just the way we are. Greeting, I have said, is a way of acknowledging one another. Ideally, this can be a form of accepting each other with no preconditions except the single fact of one's humanness. The opposite of this is selective friendship: I will speak to or greet only those who meet all of my conditions for friendship (e.g., white, middle class, educated, Southerner, Protestant, clean).

Friendship begins with the first step: acceptance. The greeting level is where this begins. A sincere greeting ("Hi there; how are you?") is acceptance, the fertile soil of a beginning friendship. It conveys the simple truth that you are important—you are of value. We usually think that rejection has to be direct and overt: telling a person "get lost" or "I don't like you." However, rejection can also be conveyed by simply ignoring a person, refusing to speak to or greet, or looking the other way. Subtle rejection can be almost as painful as direct rejection. You keep wondering why you're being ignored. A friendly "hello" can often change those feelings.

Acceptance is the basis for friendship. Greeting acknowledges the presence and importance of one another, and this conveys acceptance. This acceptance is the matrix for a growing friendship. Unconditional acceptance means that I have no plans for your improvement. I perceive you to be of great value just the way you are. I recognize you as a person in your own right. I invite you to be an important part of my life. I would like to tell you more about myself, and I trust you will reciprocate.

Recognition: The Magic Second Look

Greeting can also mean recognizing each other. Re-cognition is to know again. Recognition is a kind of magic second look, as if one is saying by his greeting, "Hey, I know you," or "Hello, don't I know you from somewhere?" To speak to someone is a form of recognition, not altogether related to having met before (although that may be the case); it is a kind of honoring the presence of someone. You are important enough to be recognized, to be greeted. You deserve my attention.

Having worked with all kinds of people, I am convinced that being recognized is a basic human need. Some feel a deeper need for recognition than others. Some are even ravenous for it and will do almost anything to get it.

In one of my pastorates, the founding pastor, then pastor emeritus, and his wife were still members there. They were truly delightful people and always my devoted supporters. However, the wife of this beloved pastor had a deep childlike craving for recognition, especially in public. Every time the two of them would make a trip out of town, she would see to it that the local newspaper published a story about their trip. The significance of the trip really didn't matter. There was a story about them in the newspaper almost every week. She made certain of that. These events, trips, and engagements were not trivial to her. Anything she did was important and deserved the widest publicity. It was the same way with her involvement in the church. I was simply glad to recognize her achievements. She worked that much harder! I guess I enjoyed recognizing her as much as she enjoyed being recognized.

Most people aren't that extreme, but everyone enjoys being recognized. Be honest. It's really nice to be recognized. It's an enjoyable and pleasant experience. Have you ever had someone unexpectedly call out your name in a crowded shopping mall in a big city several miles from home? I have. I enjoyed it. It made me feel important to be recognized when I didn't expect to be. Being ignored and overlooked is an affront to the value of our existence. Recognition affirms our worth.

Greeting can be a form of affirmation. The value of one's personhood is being recognized. One of my colleagues is the kind of man whose morning greeting, when we come into our office building, is of such a nature that it makes me feel important, valuable, and affirmed. It's not just his words but the smile on his face and the tone of his voice. A former dean of mine would greet people with a strong and confident "good morning" and a firm handclasp if not a jovial bear hug. Talk about affirmation! That made me feel like I was the most important person he had greeted that day. To affirm someone literally means "to make one strong" (i.e., firm). Certain types of greeting can do that.

The affirming type of greeting can also be an encouragement toward developing greater self-worth. As a pastor of all kinds of people and as a teacher of all kinds of students, I rarely have found an abundance of people who have a healthy sense of self-worth. It is sad that some Christians have been taught that the deeper levels of spirituality require one to develop a strong sense of self-deprecation, which results in a negative self-image. I've never read in the New Testament that Jesus ever denigrated Himself, and He's supposed to be our example.

If I am of worth to you and your greeting to me conveys that, it's bound to make a significant difference in the way I feel about myself. If others believe I am of value, then I am encouraged to value myself. Greeting has the potential to encourage.

The Dangers of Going No Deeper

The greeting level plays an important role in human relationships. It has several positive functions. However, there are several dangers to be noticed when we go no deeper with anyone. There are some people who rarely go any deeper in their relationships with others.

This can happen even in a marriage. In my last pastorate I was speaking one Sunday about the levels of relating and had just explained the greeting level when the wife of one of our couples leaned over to my wife and whispered, "That's where my husband and I are." In the morning, they greeted each other, dressed, ate breakfast, and dashed off to work. In the evening, they returned home, greeted each other, ate dinner, watched television, and then retired to bed. Communication rarely went deeper than this level, except when they argued. That couple is divorced today.

One can get locked into any of the shallower levels with only an occasional probe into a deeper level. I'm thinking primarily of people who spend most of their time on the greeting level. They may be friendly and cordial but carefully avoid going deeper.

There are definite relational limits to the greeting level. Life's greatest joys and deepest satisfactions are not to be found on this level. You certainly won't learn much about yourself or others on this level. Friendships will tend to be surface and short-lived if this is as far as you go. People need more than acknowledgment, recognition, and occasional verbal affirmation. One needs to hear more than just her name and a hello. Even computers can be programed to operate on a greeting level, and humans are more than computers.

I know a man who is very good at meeting people. He can introduce people at a party in all sorts of cute and entertaining ways. In public he's even something of an extrovert. However, if you try to get any closer to him in private or in a small group, forget it. He's friendly but has no close friends. He has misplaced his priorities. This is the way he learned to relate and get ahead in his business. But he has probably never asked a serious question or sought a serious answer in his adult life. His priorities simply do not include forming friendships on any level deeper than greeting.

Some people stay on the greeting level in order to cover up something in their past or in their personality. They find it easier to hide behind a smile and a cheery greeting than to open up their inner feelings. It's as if they're saying, "Hello, but don't come any closer." They don't want anyone to know the "ugly truth." In most cases, these persons have a very negative self-image. They lock into the greeting level because, as one student told me, "I don't like me and you won't either." He had chosen to freeze in self-negation. Oftentimes the so-called ugly truth is not nearly as bad as the person imagines. One can have a blown-up conception of his "no-goodness." We all have our dark side. Hiding it is no solution.

People who are frozen at the greeting level need to be rescued from themselves. This is a difficult point. What right do I have to rescue a person from her decision to avoid deep relationships? Do I have a messianic complex? I have discovered that some of these people desperately want to be rescued from shallowness but don't know how to ask for help. Some people are extremely shy. Their natural long-held fears are deep. But as they enter adulthood, they want more than greeting-level friends. Some have been through difficult times (loss of parents, job, mate) and realize that when the going gets rough, you need more than to be known, recognized, and greeted. You need some deep-rooted relationships. So I guess it is important for someone to reach out to these people, or they will go on being isolated. So often, the "Hello, I'm fine" just isn't true.

What Do You Say after You Say Hello?

How do you go deeper than the greeting level? What do you say after you say hello?[1]

First of all, you have to recognize the need to go deeper. The sad truth for many is that they don't know that there are deeper levels and that they've never gone, at least rarely and not for long, any deeper than level 2. Are you aware that you are locked into this level?

Second, you have to commit yourself to spend some time with people probing for the deeper levels. You will need to search for potential friends who have similar interests and needs and who are looking for friends too. You have to be willing to get involved in other people's lives, in their homes, in their recreation, and (what better place?) in their church activities. This takes planning, time, and commitment.

Third, you have to make the effort. Invite someone to lunch or dinner. If you have a family, invite another family over to your house for pizza or popcorn. Find a church and participate in its activities. No one can do this for you. Decide what's important and go after it.

If most of your relationships are at the greeting level, you have been missing the time of your life. Nothing is as exciting as making new friends, which is like discovering new worlds—everyone brings his or her world of experience into a friendship. Every time I come to do research at Oxford, I meet and make new friends from all over the world. I usually eat in the Regent's Park dining room because there I have an opportunity each weekday to develop these new friendships. It has been a most rewarding experience. We share not only our academic interests but our personal hopes and dreams as well. Remaining aloof would be such a waste and tragedy with all these wonderful people around.

I like the telephone commercial on television: "Reach out and touch someone." This is so much more than a commercial. Reaching out is

1. See Eric Berne, *What Do You Say After You Say Hello?* (New York: Bantam, 1975), chapter 1.

a lifesaver for many who truly want to go deeper than the greeting level. Look around you—where you work, where you live, where you play—and try to spot someone who needs your friendship. Reach out. Go deeper.

5

The Search for a Reason
to Be Friends

The greeting level is only the first step, the opening of the door in the search for friendship. Two people don't just accidentally become friends. They have to have a reason or, to be realistic, several reasons. We will now examine the search for a reason to be friends. In this chapter, I will discuss the next two levels of relationships: level 3, the separate-interests level, and level 4, the common-interests level. Both of these are more conversational and informational levels than they are actional levels. Friendship is more than talk but friendship is born in talk.

Going Beyond the Greeting Level

For the past several days I have been politely greeting one of the research guests here at Regent's Park College in the library, in the dining hall, or simply as we passed in the halls or on the streets. This evening after dinner I had the wonderful opportunity of getting to know on a deeper level Pastor Horst Niesen of Hamburg, West Germany. We are about the same age with similar pastoral backgrounds. He is at Oxford studying conversational English. Having coffee together in the Senior Common Room, we went beyond the greeting

71

level as we discovered that, although he comes from West Germany and I from the United States, we have a lot in common. I plan to keep in touch with this man. He has a lot to teach me and us at the school where I teach, and maybe we can be of help to him and his work. In a few months he will become the executive leader of the European Baptist Mission Society. He plans to visit our campus in the near future. I believe that a friendship has been born. We decided to go beyond the greeting level and it was a good experience.

One has to be dissatisfied with spending so much time in shallow relationships if one is going to go any deeper. Many contacts in church are on such a level, and no wonder a lot of people feel they get nothing from going to church on Sunday. There has to be a growing conviction that there is more to life than a smile and a nod of the head if one is going to develop close friendships. I had at least two roommates in college whom I never really got to know, and yet we were cordial to each other. We were never really dissatisfied enough with a shallow relationship to go beyond the greeting level. As I think back, all three of us were confused and frustrated young men in need of deep relationships but were too afraid to reach out to each other.

To go beyond the greeting level with someone, you need to feel strongly that "I need a friend and you need a friend too, so let's check out the possibilities." This may sound selfish but it really isn't. If we need each other, and we have something vital to give to each other, that's not selfishness. That's just plain commonsense awareness of our mutual need.

As I think about how this applies to marriage, I realize I need a wife who does more than fulfill certain wifely roles—homemaker, cook, second-income earner, sex partner, family social-life director, and mother of my children. I need a wife who is a friend. Likewise, she needs a husband who is more than a major breadwinner, house and car fix-it man, protector, and father of her children. She needs a husband who is a friend.

In the 1950 movie, *Shenandoah*, the father of the family around which the plot is built was played by Jimmy Stewart. You may recall a young man asking him for his daughter's hand in marriage. The father asks the young man why he wants to marry her, to which he replies, "Because I love her." The father retorts, "But do you like her?" The young fellow is puzzled. "Like her? Well, I guess so." The father concludes, "There is a difference, you know." A good marriage needs more than good role-performers and lovers. It needs good friends who know they need each other.

To go beyond the greeting level, you have to explore each other's interests to see if you have anything to share. Friendships are built upon commonalities. To explore takes effort, time from other concerns, and conversation: asking questions about one's interests. Looking for a friend is like digging for gold. You have to work at it. Many times, the effort turns up nothing. But sometimes you strike it rich.

When my wife and I began dating, we discovered that we had several things in common in addition to being physically and socially attracted to each other: the same educational goals and the same church preference and attendance. We enjoyed the same kind of movies (there was little else to do in our hometown). Both of us sang in the church choir, held the same religious and moral values, and were interested in marriage and a family (not discussed at first, of course). In time we discovered other commonalities. These discoveries provided the foundation for our developing relationship. This took a lot of talking, asking questions, and self-disclosure, and that took a lot of time and seeing each other.

What if this exploration into each other's life turns up not common interests but separate interests? If there are few or no commonalities, then the relationship will probably go nowhere. I believe that for a friendship to develop there must be some commonalities. But separate interests will show up. Then what? At some point a decision will have to be made.

Are there enough common interests, especially values, to sustain the relationship? If so, then you have to decide whether you can or want to learn from each other in regard to your separate interests. There can be something very healthy about discovering separate interests. These can be the means for getting out of the ruts of the past. You can learn a lot from the interests of others. If I had chosen to freeze in my own interests, I would never have learned anything about art, music, skiing (both water and snow), photography, or travel.

Conversation Begins the Search

In the search for a reason to be friends, conversation begins the process. You can't just stick to yourself and wait for someone else to pull you into a relationship. You start by telling people who you are and what you're like, along with asking a lot of questions: who are you and what are you like? The separate- and common-interests levels are actually informational levels. You are discovering specific things about specific people.

When I refer to interests, I am suggesting several possible categories: tastes, attractions, concerns, involvements, commitments, and values. Obviously, these all overlap to some extent in anyone's life.

Tastes are one's likings, preferences, predilections. Tastes include not only certain activities but also a certain quality of activity. When I say I have a taste for preaching, I don't mean just any preaching. There is nothing quite as bad as bad preaching. The same applies to public worship in general. During the last two Sundays here in Oxford, I have heard three different sermons. One (by Michael Green) was superb: uplifting, inspiring, effectively illustrated, full of life and excitement, mixed with appropriate humor and examples from real situations—all of this in addition to biblical soundness. The other two (by preachers who will remain unnamed, naturally) were wretched: dull, lifeless, irrelevant, antiquated. Both men frowned and scowled much more than they smiled, and I had the feeling they really weren't aware of that. A kind of negativism prevailed throughout their messages. But then, all of this is a matter of taste. I'm telling you more about myself than I am about three preachers.

I have a taste for certain kinds of food, literature, and music. I am also interested in certain attractions: sports, movies, plays, television programs, to mention a few. I have an interest in certain concerns: issues in the political, economic, educational, and religious arenas.

I have certain involvements. Among all of my tastes, attractions, and concerns, only certain ones engage my time and presence. Here is where I become active: attending meetings, joining organizations, participating directly, taking risks, giving money. These engagements also reflect my commitments: what I am willing to pay for, be present for, go out of my way for, be willing to sacrifice for. These will also tell you what my values are: what I esteem and greatly prize, the goals I am willing to pursue, the objectives I wish to accomplish, even what I am willing to die for.

My interests will tell you a great deal about who and what I am. To the degree that these are the same in our lives, to this degree we hold life in common. If our interests are greatly different, we may not have much to talk about, not for long at least. Now we have to talk about these interests if we are to get to know each other.

Someone must take the initiative. If I choose to do so, then I will try to tell you what I am (the "who" comes later). I will want to tell you what I think: my beliefs, whether they be about the accuracy of weather forecasters or political ideology or my personal religious convictions. My attitudes will also come through as I talk: my prejudices (I've learned that everyone is prejudiced about something; the only difference is that some of us have our prejudices under control better than others); my feelings toward certain people (my next-door neighbors) or certain roles (preachers and politicians). I will also reveal my values (people are more important than things, time is more valuable than money, children are of greater value than pets or flowers, family is of more significance than career).

I will tell you a lot about what I do: where I go to work and what I do there; my hobbies or recreational activities; the church I attend with my family; my weekend agenda; what I do in my spare time (one of the most revealing things I will tell you).

If time permits I will tell you about what I want in life: my goals, objectives, desires. This list can get quite long: an expensive sports car or a camper, a larger house in a more exclusive neighborhood or a cabin on a lake, the ideal number of children or maybe none at all, the kind of husband or wife, the kind of job or career I seek, and finally (no pun intended) the plans I'm making for retirement.

If you are perceptive enough, maybe you will learn something very revealing about me, and that is what I give: to what do I contribute freely and how generously. This includes not only my money but also my time and, most importantly, myself. To what and to whom do I give my presence, influence, and participation? One's giving habits reveal one's innermost convictions.

All of this will tell you something of what I am, what kind of person I am in action. I trust this revelation will cause you to reciprocate in kind.

Therefore, I am interested in learning what you are: what you think—your beliefs, your attitudes, your feelings, and your values. I also trust you will tell me what you do: your job activities, recreational interests, religious behavior, what you do in your spare time.

Likewise, what do you want in and from life: goals and desires, property and people, finances and future, hopes and dreams. Possibly I can also discover what you really believe is of value by what you give and how generous you are, and whether you consider your money or your self more important as you give. To whom or what you give will also be revealing.

Discovering Separate Interests

Our early interchanges may reveal our interests are more separate than similar. Of course, this is a matter of degree. No two people are totally different, nor are they totally alike. When my wife and I are angry with each other over something said or done, usually one of us says, "Well, it just goes to show that we have absolutely nothing in common." Then when our feelings for each other are warm and affectionate, you would think we have everything in common. Emotions have a lot to do with mutual attraction or the lack of it.

If our conversations reveal that most of our interests diverge rather than converge, then we are discovering that in the more crucial matters of life we don't think very much alike, we don't do very many of the same things, we don't want many of the same things, and we don't give many of the same things to many of the same causes or for many of the same reasons.

If you're a Democrat and I'm a Republican, if you prefer indoor activities while I prefer outdoor sports, if you're a Protestant and I'm Jewish or Catholic, if you enjoy classical music while I prefer country or mood music (what my children call "elevator music"), if you prefer the New American Standard Bible while I read the New International Version, if you drink coffee and I don't, if you contribute generously to Moral Majority and I give substantially to my local church, if you read novels most of the time while I read only the sports page of the newspaper, if you hate children and I like them, then we're not very likely to develop a close friendship. We're more likely to go our separate ways (diverge) than walk together (converge).

At some point you and I will have to decide what to do about the fact that our separate interests prevail over any meaningful common interests. Where do we go from here? First, we can simply part ways. We see no significant reason to keep the relationship going. We may perceive that we bore each other. We may wish to spend our time developing relationships with others.

Second, we may choose to not exactly part ways but only to greet when we see each other. We will be friendly but not friends. There is a difference. I sometimes hear someone say, "Oh, he's a friend of mine" when a name is mentioned, but what is meant is that these people have met or are friendly to each other. They are not truly friends. That word, it seems to me, is losing its meaning for us. From the separate-interests level, we may choose to return to the greeting level and go no further.

Third, we can choose to remain on the separate-interests level and learn new things from each other. You can teach me your interests, and I can teach you mine. This might lead to new interests for each of us that in time could become common interests. For example, in my last pastorate several families in the church enjoyed snow skiing at our nearby community ski slope above Los Alamos, New Mexico. I had never skiied before. At the age of forty-five I decided to give it a try. The others taught me. I learned something new, although I never was very good at it. I discovered the exhilaration of skiing alone through the soft snow amidst the quiet pine forests at eighty-five hundred feet altitude. Have you ever stopped in the middle of a snow-covered forest and listened to the muffled sounds of nature? It's almost a religious experience. What a contrast to the clanging noises of the concrete jungle of an urban center. I'll always be glad I learned a new sport from those whose interests at first were different from mine.

Learning new interests is very important in keeping life vibrant, exciting, challenging, and growing. If you always choose to stay within the limits of common interests, watch out for the monster called Boredom—he may move in someday and eat your lunch. I have learned the importance of maintaining a healthy balance of common and separate interests in my relationships with others.

Whatever we choose—to part ways, revert to the greeting level, or learn from each other—will depend upon our levels of maturity and security. If we choose to learn from each other, I believe we are expressing a deeper level of maturity and expressing a deeper sense of security. However, it isn't always the case that we ought to maintain every relationship where separate interests prevail. Our values may seriously clash and make it impossible to go on relating meaningfully (e.g., if you're a thief and I want to obey the law), but we ought to be open enough to see what the possibilities are.

Developing Friends Who Differ from Us

I want to make a case for developing friends among those who are different from us. Especially Christians in the church do not reach out enough to people whose interests and values are not those of Christians. As a consequence, many churches become religious ghettos.

I realize there is a major obstacle here—the will of the other person.

He may not want your friendship, for you are different from him too. There are things about you that bother him. If he's a factory worker and you're a middle-class businessman, then he may immediately think that you're a stuffy, egotistical prude of a fellow. Forget it, he would say. He hasn't time for killjoys.

However, if you're a Christian, you try to reach out anyhow because there's something more important involved here than what each of you initially thinks of the other. In the long run, relationships are more than cultural traits, social-class characteristics, personal habits, economic variables, educational backgrounds, and religious practices. Relationships have a spiritual quality: two or more human spirits discovering that they have more common interests than they do differences, that differences are often more superficial than we think, that at the core of our being we have historically a common source, potentially a common purpose, and (we hope) a common destiny. There is often even a mystical dimension in relationships whereby two people hit it off for no apparent reason.

I want to propose several suggestions for developing friends among those who are different from us.

First of all, if you are different from me, I will need to give you the right to be different. Actually, you already have that right, and I need to recognize it. I must accept your differentness if we are to be friends. Likewise, you will need to accept me as I am. There must be no plans for the other's improvement, no hidden agenda to change the other. I don't have the right to make you over into my image. I doubt seriously if I could do that if I wanted to.

The quickest way to destroy a budding relationship is to set in to convert or change the other to fit some preconceived notion. I often see this in marital relationships: a woman marries a man believing she can change him into the ideal (her ideal, of course) husband after the wedding. This is pure folly. It just doesn't work. You can't change someone else. You can only change yourself. Trying to change the other will usually ruin a potentially good relationship.

Many of the conflicts my wife and I have had through the years have been in this regard. When Carole and I finally learned to accept our differences, we then discovered a foundation for building a lasting and enjoyable relationship. For one thing, we stopped expending so much energy trying to manipulate the other into changing into each other's own image. Also, we stopped getting angry over our failures to change the other, which was very exhausting.

The second step in developing friends who are different is an open commitment to share our differences. Again, this is a two-way street. Let's openly and honestly share our beliefs, opinions, and convictions and *why* they are held. This applies across the board: religion, politics, family life, sex, morality.

I developed a close friendship with a student of mine from Saudi Arabia when I was teaching sociology at Hardin-Simmons University. Adel Shaben was Arab, Muslim, fifteen years younger than I, and unmarried. Our differences far exceeded our commonalities. Yet, in our conversations in my office, in the student center, or in walking across the campus we shared our differences openly and honestly. We consequently learned a great deal about each other and our respective cultures and a friendship grew. At his graduation I gave him a copy of the New Testament in Arabic. He was deeply touched, and we embraced. He returned to his native country to work in his government's police force (his degree was in law enforcement). If we were to meet again, our friendship would quickly rekindle. We were far apart in so many ways yet very close in spirit, which is the basis for meaningful relationships.

In my last pastorate, I found myself often frustrated over how to lead people at opposite ends of the theological spectrum to develop close relationships. When people at the extremes identify themselves as fundamentalists or liberals they usually create a major problem for themselves, for they're prone to see those who differ with them as theological "enemies." This means it's difficult for those people to become friends. That is so unfortunate and unnecessary. I have found people at both extremes to be very insecure.

The healthiest atmosphere for developing friendships among people of extreme theological differences is one of mutual respect and an open and honest sharing of differences whereby both can learn from each other. It would be helpful if we'd all stop labeling each other and make an honest effort to get to know each other. Truth is not found in labels but in relationships. Jesus said, "I [not a creed or confession] am . . . the truth" (John 14:6). God is neither a fundamentalist nor a liberal. He abhors labels and so do I. Mere labeling is a lazy person's way out of the hard search for truth, which is always found in the matrix of relationships.

The third step in developing friends who are different is an open commitment to learn from our differences. I never met a person I couldn't learn something from. I don't have to agree, but I can expand my knowledge of others and their ways if I'll commit myself to making the effort.

All three of my children are different and they are very different from me. It's difficult to understand how we came out of the same family. Yet I have learned much from each of them. For example, my daughter, Paige, is somewhat small in size. From her I have learned something of the pain and difficulty of being undesirably small in a society that expects you to be of normal size—whatever that is—and reminds you of your "abnormality" in every department store or school activity. From my older son, Nelson, I have learned something of the temperament and concern for detail of the art world. From my younger son, Todd, I have learned about cows, horses, chickens, and things mechanical. As we learn more about our differences, I believe we are growing closer together.

Fourth, it certainly helps to discover that friendships are of more value than our separate interests. You and I are more important than what we are interested in and what we do as a result of those interests. Our culture conditions us to believe that we *are* what we *do*, or that we are valuable only in terms of what we do. I believe there is a given value in simply being human.

In certain instances, I have developed some very close friendships with people who were quite different from me in interests and activities. One of the closest friends I ever had was T. P. Byrum, a man who ran a dry cleaning establishment in my hometown. He was several years older than I. We rarely did anything together. One time, when I was seventeen years old, we were a part of a group of men who went trout fishing in Colorado for a week. T. P. was a deacon and an active leader in our church. We saw each other mostly in church on Sundays or whenever I took clothes into his place to be cleaned. Although he and his wife Bea were close friends of my parents, I was never, as far as I can remember, in his home.

T. P. was a practical joker of the neatest sort, was a lot of fun to be around, had a keen wit, was personable to the nth degree, and truly cared about people. In more ways than not, we were very different, yet he was a very close friend, and I always felt it when I was around him; and I still do when I return home to visit relatives in Frederick. him, and, still do when I return home to visit relatives in Frederick. I'll always remember that every time I would preach in my home church, T. P. would come up after the benediction and say, "Guy, that was the finest sermon I ever heard." Although I didn't believe a word of it (his remarks, not my sermon), I knew he was trying to affirm me, and I'll always be grateful. So different were we, yet so close.

In developing friendships and closeness with people with separate interests, one must beware of certain dangers. One can go too far, morally and spiritually. As a Christian, I am committed to a certain ethical stance. There are certain things I am clearly forbidden by Scripture to do, certain associations I must avoid, not because I am better than or holier than anyone else, but because of the very nature of certain behavior which expresses a rebellion against God and which would involve harming myself and others.

This position is clearly set forth in 2 Corinthians 6:14–7:1 (NIV).

Do not be yoked together with unbelievers. For what do righteousness and wickedness have in common? Or what fellowship can light have with darkness? What harmony is there between Christ and Belial? What does a believer have in common with an unbeliever? What agreement is there between the temple of God and idols? For we are the temple of the living God. As God has said: "I will live with them and walk among them, and I will be their God, and they will be my people."

"Therefore come out from them
   and be separate,
                                          says the Lord.

Touch no unclean thing,
   and I will receive you."
"I will be a Father to you,
   and you will be my sons and daughters,
                                          says the Lord Almighty."

Since we have these promises, dear friends, let us purify ourselves from everything that contaminates body and spirit, perfecting holiness out of reverence for God.

We have already discussed the difficult balance of penetration and separation in the Christian life (chap. 3). I must not compromise my moral convictions nor water down my theological beliefs in order to maintain certain friendships. Friendships are of greater value than interests, but my relationship and commitment to God as well as my personal integrity are of greater value than any friendship here on earth.

For instance, if I'm going to be friends with people who frequent bars, I'll visit them in their places of work or in their homes, not in the bars they frequent (unless there are unusual circumstances that call for an exception). Jesus was occasionally called "a drunkard," probably because He associated with drinkers. He was also called a friend of tax collectors and sinners. He was not above relating to such people (Matt. 11:19; Luke 7:34). Yet He never surrendered His moral and spiritual integrity to do so.

Discovering Common Interests

The fourth level of relating I have identified as the common-interests level. This is going deeper, for you will get closer to people on this level. This is still a conversational and informational level. If in a crowd of strangers you find someone with whom you have interests in common, certain internal bells ring and lights flash. Common interests may range from children to jobs to home state, to religious affiliation or faith, to language, to education or school attended, to sports, to literature, to music, to age, to race, to ethnic identity. The possibilities are as broad as your interests.

When two people discover they have more common interests than separate ones, they feel attracted to each other because their common interests are the result of common backgrounds and experiences. One's particular location in the class system of society largely predetermines what is seen, perceived, felt, and experienced in daily living. Two people from the same class will, therefore, tend to see life in the same way and think alike. People who live in the same neighborhood (or type of neighborhood), go to the same schools, play on the same sports team, or go to the same church will feel that they have common interests. They come out of the same social world.

People who have had similar experiences will also feel a mutual attraction: both served in the military, both have been married about twenty years, their mates have died, both are divorced, both have a drinking problem, both have nursery-age children, both attended a Billy Graham crusade last month and were converted, both left the Episcopal church to become Presbyterians, both got lost in traffic on the way to the new shopping mall, both recently sent a son or daughter off to college for the first time, or both have an unemployed husband. Common experiences have a way of drawing people together.

A major part of the dynamic of attraction is that there is security, or at least a feeling of it, in similarity. From studies about attraction, some psychologists have developed what they call a reinforcement-affect theory, which relates to common interests.[1] If a person with whom you are relating holds the same values, attitudes, beliefs, and opinions that you hold, that person validates or confirms your version of social reality. In this confirmation the person with these commonalities tends to bolster your sense of competence in dealing with and explaining the social world you live in. This similarity provides a certain satisfaction in your ability to function meaningfully with others.

Dissimilarity is likely to be threatening to your definition of life and may call into question your ability to deal with life. Such a negative arousal can be very uncomfortable. One way of reducing any unpleasantness is to avoid the person who is different.

Because security is a basic need of all people, it is only natural to be attracted to people who have interests common to yours. This is most often seen at a party: women bunch up with women, and men group with men because of sex-role commonalities. The sports enthusiasts gather in one group and the political zealots in another. The young mothers form one group and the middle-aged career women another. This is the movement toward security.

In common interests we meet ourselves. If I am honest, I will admit that, as far as I'm concerned, I'm the most important person in the world. I know this is self-centeredness, but it is also the way I feel. My way of thinking, believing, and acting is the best way. Now this is all in my head. I both believe it and disbelieve it. So I need a lot of confirmation that my perception, emotions, and conclusions are correct. If I can find others who agree with me, this reinforces the way I feel. Consequently, I feel better. In relating to people who have interests common to mine, I meet myself and find that needed reinforcement. I come away from such relationships feeling, "Hey, I was right after all!" In a similar way I come away feeling, "Boy, am I glad I'm not alone in all this business called life."

When I relate to people who have interests common to mine, it means that we tend to think alike. We hold a similar body of knowledge. We reason much the same way. We believe a great deal alike (this applies to religion, philosophy, customs, practices, and reality in general). We have similar attitudes and opinions. We hold similar values.

Values are probably the most important variable in common interests. Values are those goals (material or nonmaterial) we consider

1. Clyde Hendrick and Susan Hendrick, *Liking, Loving, and Relating* (Monterey, CA: Brooks/Cole, 1983), pp. 24–26.

worth pursuing in life: whatever is prized or esteemed and worth seeking, achieving, or possessing. Values are one's principles or standards, one's judgments as to what is important or significant in life. Therefore, humans are attracted to those who have common values, whether those values concern money, status, character, land, or position. We are most comfortable when we're associating with people who hold values similar to ours.

When I relate to people who hold interests common to mine, it probably means that we do some of the same things or act in similar ways. Since our actions are so often social, requiring others (e.g., whether pooling our investment funds or playing tennis), we can work together in these common activities for our mutual betterment or enjoyment.

We also tend to want the same things. We can learn from each other how better to reach these similar goals (e.g., whether a job, or marriage and a family, or spiritual growth). Moreover, having common interests, we tend to give the same things (whether time or money or self) to the same needs (whether church or home or the poor) for the same reasons (whether compassion or duty or guilt).

Building a Friendship upon Common Interests

I have found that people will build true friendships upon common interests as the initial foundation rather than upon any other ground (such as expertise, availability, or influence).

God has made us in such a way that it is natural to look for friends within familiar territory. The family was the matrix of our early growth and development. Friendships are but extensions of the family. Consequently, we look for friends among "home folk," people much like us. There is nothing wrong with this as long as it is seen as only a beginning in developing a wide range of friends to whom we relate on varying levels.

Church-growth mission strategists debate which is the more Christian method of evangelism: emphasizing the principle of homogeneity or the principle of heterogeneity. The former states that churches grow best and fastest if they seek to reach only one class of people (i.e., those with common interests and backgrounds); the latter contends that churches ought to grow as a mix of all kinds of people (i.e., those with separate interests and differing backgrounds). The first is seen as a sociological principle, whereas the second is based upon a biblical-theological-ethical model. Both principles have elements of truth. The first is based upon reality; the second envisions the kingdom of God, which will include all kinds of people (Luke 13:29). By analogy, I contend that friendships have to begin with common interests. One's ability to form friendships, however, ought to grow to the extent that one can reach out to people of separate interests.

If we're going to build a friendship upon our common interests, then these interests have to be shared. This primarily means that we will share our previous experiences. When I wrote *The Wounded Parent*,[2] I had no idea that so many people would respond via letters and phone calls. These were wounded parents who wished to talk or correspond about our common interest: relating to a morally and spiritually wayward son or daughter. I had shared some of my experiences in the book, and now others were wanting to share their experiences with me. In addition, numerous churches requested that my wife and I lead retreats or conferences on parenting, with special emphasis on wounded parents. As we shared our experiences, other parents would share theirs. As a result, several new friendships have developed. Our common interest in parenting has brought us together.

Even when common interests bring us together, we make an obvious discovery: we're not exactly alike. I say "obvious" because we ought to know that some differences are bound to exist. As I mentioned earlier, my wife and I were initially drawn together to a great extent by our common interests. Yet through the years of our marriage we have discovered, oftentimes painfully so and oftentimes pleasurably so, that we are not exactly alike. There are distinct differences.

On the negative side, I discovered that Carole would often, as I perceived the problem, try to dominate the family situation. She was reared to believe that the mother is to be in charge of the family. I was taught that the father should be. I found that at times she preferred to be a loner, spending much time in private, doing private kinds of things (e.g., sewing). I married her not to encourage isolation, but to be *with* her, doing things together. Early in the marriage, she had great difficulty overtly expressing affection. I craved affection. Also, she had some deep-rooted inhibitions regarding sex. Her culture had taught her the unbiblical concept of sex as something shameful, dirty, and never to be enjoyed. I felt just the opposite: sex in marriage

2. Guy Greenfield, *The Wounded Parent: Coping with Parental Discouragement* (Grand Rapids: Baker, 1982).

should be wholesome, enjoyable, rewarding, loving, and pleasurable, as the Bible so clearly teaches. In addition, she lived in another world when it came to money: money is earned to be spent, not saved. I was very conservative (and anxious) about finances. My ancestors came from Scotland! These differences created some serious problems that took several years of re-education and adjustment to resolve.

On the positive side, I discovered that Carole is a marvelous connoisseur of food. She is a *supérieure cuisinière* of the most delectable dishes. I am a disaster at cooking. Moreover, I found her to be a fantastic hostess who loves to entertain in the home. I am a Neanderthal in such matters. In addition, she can sing beautifully. I can hardly carry a tune. Also, she is an immaculate housekeeper. I never learned the first thing about that, for my mother always picked up after me. Carole reads novels; I rarely look at one, although I enjoy a good story or plot. You'll have to ask her about my positive features—I can't think of any right now. I've said all of this to point out that our differences became the means for enriching our lives. Responding positively to our differences often provided the serendipitous elements of our marriage.

In spite of the enrichment that diversity can provide within relationships, it is nevertheless the commonalities within a friendship that provide the basis for not only attraction to each other but also support for each other. One basic purpose for developing a friendship is to gain support in and for one's endeavors: encouragement and affirmation are to the mind and heart what vitamins and minerals are to the body.

It helps me to know that my view of reality is legitimate. As we share our common interests and perspectives, and enjoy doing so, I find the legitimation that undergirds my experience of reality. It helps to know that I'm not odd, for someone else shares some or most of my interests and together we affirm each other in those interests.

Moreover, I have discovered that among those friends with whom I share certain common interests will be some who become my very close friends. Some will go with me beyond mere conversation to the level of doing things together (level 5: social interaction), and some will go with me even to deeper levels: caring, sharing, and intimacy. At these deeper levels, even greater support will be experienced.

The Biblical Basis for Christian Commonality

As we discuss the idea of sharing things in common, it is interesting to notice that a key word in the New Testament refers to commonality:

koinōnia, a Greek word that is usually translated "fellowship." It literally means a sharing of that which is held in common, which could refer to either food or faith, property or love, money or hope.

A pertinent passage is Acts 2:42–47 (NIV).

> They [the new believers at Pentecost] devoted themselves to the apostles' teaching and to the fellowship *(koinōnia),* to the breaking of bread and to prayer. Everyone was filled with awe, and many wonders and miraculous signs were done by the apostles. All the believers were together and had everything in common *(koina).* Selling their possessions and goods, they gave to anyone as he had need. Every day they continued to meet together in the temple courts. They broke bread in their homes and ate together with glad and sincere hearts, praising God and enjoying the favor of all the people. And the Lord added to their number daily those who were being saved.

Notice that the fellowship expressed itself among the believers in several ways: a togetherness of faith, a sharing of their wealth with those in need, and a togetherness in worship of their common Lord. In spite of the diversity of these early believers (note their varied backgrounds and cultures; Acts 2:5–13), they were attracted to each other by their common faith, their common interests that centered around Jesus Christ as proclaimed in the gospel.

Other passages of relevance are 1 Corinthians 1:10–13 and 3:1–9, which point out that togetherness is an important and desirable goal for Christians in spite of obvious differences. Togetherness is achievable through a common faith in the same Lord, Jesus Christ. In 2 Corinthians 13:11–14 we read that the fellowship *(koinōnia)* of the Holy Spirit is the means whereby agreement and togetherness in relationships are possible. It is the presence of God Himself in the relationships of believers that makes Christian friendship possible. This is also taught in Ephesians 4:1–3, which refers to the "unity of the Spirit." This unity is additionally described as "fellowship *(koinōnia)* with the Spirit," which aims toward "being like-minded, having the same love, being one in spirit and purpose" (Phil. 2:1–2, NIV).

It seems to me that the common-interests level of relating is alluded to in these biblical teachings on fellowship or commonality. In the search for a reason to be friends, what greater reason could we have than that we worship the same God through a common faith in His son, Jesus Christ? Moreover, experience reveals that an amazing depth of friendship is quickly created when two Christians of diverse backgrounds and cultures meet for the first time. Why? Because there exists between and within them a participation *(koinōnia)* in the Spirit of God.

A Springboard for the Future

The common-interests level is clearly a springboard for reaching the deeper levels of relating. It is at this level, in time, that we discover those areas of our lives that we can share in common activities. There will be certain things we can do together rather than just talk about them.

Moreover, in doing things together, things that we have in common, we will have opportunities to probe for the deeper levels of relating. Surely there is more to a friendship than simply talking about things or ideas we both enjoy or agree upon. Instead of just talking about fishing, let's go fishing together. Instead of merely discussing a Shakespeare play, such as *Twelfth Night* or *Henry VIII*, let's attend one and get caught up in its dramatic moods together. I mention these in particular because my son, Nelson, and I have just returned from Stratford-upon-Avon where we attended performances of these plays in the Royal Shakespeare Theater. And most importantly, instead of simply talking about our faith in Jesus Christ among ourselves, let's go together and share it with someone.

We have so much more to share than just our interests: we have ourselves, our time, our resources, our mutual support and affirmation. For a deeper friendship to flourish, we need to move from conversation and information to action and involvement.

6

Togetherness in Action

Level 5 is the social-interaction level. On this level our friendship will center upon doing things together. This is where we serve on the same church committee, play on the same ball team, go walking together regularly in the park, go to people's homes as a church visitation team, go jogging together each morning, work together in the yard and garden each Saturday morning, go on a vacation together, sing in the same choir, go out for dinner and a movie each Friday night, or participate in a Tuesday-night domino group or a Monday-night Bible-study group. Notice how togetherness, common participation, regularity, and mutual experience, in addition to some meaningful conversation, are all found in the action at this level.

Going Beyond Conversation

If we are going to go any deeper than the common-interests level of relating, then we must go beyond conversation to *experience* our commonality.

We must not forget that talking and listening are important and will continue at level 5. We all need to verbalize our interests, feelings, explanations, hopes, dreams, disappointments, victories, aspirations, and goals. And somebody needs to listen to us with what my friend

Doug Manning calls that magical "laying on of ears."[1] Folks need to believe that at least one person in this world will listen to and understand them. However. . . .

Action is better. Action is talk with shoes on it. Social interaction is conversation engaged in meaningful participation. Some may argue that conversation is action, and to a degree that is true. It is action through verbal symbols. However, words can never take the place of certain forms of behavior: for example, talking about God (theology) versus worshiping God or leading someone into a personal relationship with God through faith in Jesus Christ; talking about marriage versus actually getting married; talking about childbirth versus having a baby yourself; discussing the tennis matches at Wimbleton versus playing a game of tennis yourself.

I am reminded of Søren Kierkegaard's story of an old French eccentric who spent hours memorizing pages of railroad timetables and discussing them with his friends at the train station. But never once did he ride a train. Recently, I preached in a church where there were more than five hundred decisions made. More than five hundred people decided not to do one thing I had talked about! If the American church ever dies, it will die of talkitis and lack of exercise. Many a friendship grows stale on all words and no action. Many a marriage dies because of no action.

Closeness in personal relationships requires togetherness if any significant depth is to be reached. However, togetherness is more than merely being together, in proximity, under the same roof or in the same car. It means sharing in a common activity. I have observed many marriages that have grown cool because couples have gradually stopped doing anything meaningful together. Their "togetherness" amounts to sitting together for hours in front of a television set, even eating most of their at-home meals there rather than in the dining room. Even in church they listen to someone else talk or perform. There is little if any real interaction between them. They are observers, spectators, not coparticipants.

I cannot know you merely from your words. I need your action in concert with mine. Through participation in a mutual endeavor we reveal a deeper part of ourselves to each other. I got to know my father best when we worked together in our family store, or when we fished

1. See Doug Manning's very helpful book, *Don't Take My Grief Away From Me* (Hereford, TX: Insight Books, 1980).

together a few yards away from each other in a trout stream and later shared our catch. Deepening relationships need active togetherness.

After we've gotten to know each other on the common-interests level and have decided to go deeper, one of us must take the initiative and suggest doing something together. This will be a sort of testing the water to see if our friendship can go further. In engaging in some common activity, we are going beyond conversation to experience our commonalities.

When Carole and I were dating we learned about our common interest in the church through long discussions, but it wasn't until we started going to nearby rural churches to lead worship services together (I preached and she sang) that we experienced our common interest. This mutual experiencing of church work brought us closer together. We still cherish the memories of that first summer we taught in a Vacation Bible School together, months before we got engaged. Those shared activities played a major role in our growing closeness.

Doing Things Together

What kinds of things can we do together to deepen and develop our relationship? I can only speak from my own experience. Each person reading this book could write his or her own chapter on this. Everyone's interests and activities are uniquely his or hers. The suggestions I'm about to make are only that—suggestions. Depending upon your background, you may think that my life is either dull or overloaded and exhausting.

In Marriage

If you're married, I'm thinking of just the two of you. Forget the children for the moment. Your activities together must be seen as priority time. What you do together is crucial time well spent. It will affect all of your other relationships and activities. First, you have to plan ahead. For example, if at all possible, plan one night out each week. Leave the children with a baby sitter or friend. Some couples take turns keeping each other's children on their respective night out to save money on baby sitters. Do what you enjoy doing as a couple: see a movie or a drama, have dinner in a relaxed atmosphere, or take a walk in the park or a shopping mall. It doesn't have to be expensive. This is time alone for just the two of you.

There may be those special places each couple enjoys going to: a park, a resort, a lake, a river, a shopping center, a restaurant, a theater, a hill overlooking the city, or a beach. In Santa Fe we enjoyed certain Spanish restaurants, or in Taos just walking through the art galleries and shops. In Albuquerque, there was Old Town, Coronado, or the State Fair.

Then don't forget those very special days, especially your wedding anniversary. It is all but unforgivable for a husband to forget his own wedding anniversary and say or do nothing about celebrating it with his wife. Harry Emerson Fosdick was fond of saying, "There is no democracy among days." Some days call for special recognition and activity: his or her birthday, Mother's Day, Father's Day, Christmas, Valentine's Day, Easter. Carole and I married on August 14, so we made a point of celebrating Valentine's Day (it was exactly a half-year anniversary for us). Doing something special together on special days has a way of enriching the relationship.

Doing special things for each other on ordinary days can be rewarding also. Surprise your mate tonight with a special dinner (in or out) when there isn't any particular occasion for doing so. I enjoyed hearing a friend of mine describe the evening he got home from work to find his wife had packed a suitcase for both of them, had deposited the children at a neighbor's house, had made a reservation at a resort hotel in a nearby city, and then drove him there for the weekend—all to his pleasant surprise and for no special reason. They still laugh about the fun they had: she in surprising him, he in being surprised, and they on the weekend away.

It's important for a married couple to play together. It's a healthy sign when we can let the "child inside us" come out to play, to romp, to laugh, to enjoy, to know the pleasure of each other's company as we do something we both enjoy. It's equally important to learn to pray together, to share your life not only with each other but also with the God who made you and brought you together in marriage. Such a routine can be both an enriching and a deepening of your relationship.

At Home with the Children

Many of you reading this book have children still at home. A few suggestions for you are in order. Interacting with members of the family in a meaningful (or necessary) activity is vital to achieving closeness. Around the house there are always several things—yardwork, cleaning, repairing, gardening, hobbies—that can be done *together*. I'll always remember the week my sons, their grandfather, and I put up about three hundred feet of fence around our back yard in Los Alamos. It was a great accomplishment for us (we'd never done anything like that before), but greater still was our working together for that week, telling stories out of the past, telling old and new jokes, and pooling our brainpower on how to build a fence, especially the gates!

Vacations can be another important time for a family. Although vacations are taken away from home, home is really wherever the family is. I will have to admit that some of our vacations were nightmares on the road: three young children in the back of a station wagon can create chaos. I've had to stop the car out on a freeway several times in my life and crawl into the back seat just to physically restore order after verbal threats became meaningless! I'll take parenting teenagers any day to handling children ages four, seven, and ten on a long trip. With small children, *always* make *short* trips! When we are going somewhere in the car, a standard joke in our family to this day is, "Daddy, are we there yet?" even if we're only thirty minutes away from the house.

Try to plan your vacations together as a family. Let everyone have some input. Of course, some ideas will have to be vetoed, for example, "Let's go to the North Pole!" It helps if certain details are explained to the children: days on the road, places for overnight stops, dos and don'ts, sights to be seen and things to be done, when to return home, and what we'll do with the dog and cat while we're away. A family council meeting can be productive and will create more cooperation.[2]

Playing together is important. I always enjoyed our times on the beach in Florida, or fishing in mountain streams in New Mexico or Colorado, or just swinging in the back yard at home. I regret that I didn't play with my children more than I did. A husband and wife ought to play together: it's good for you relationally as well as physically, but probably of equal importance is the model of play it provides for the children. If you all aren't the sporty types, then at least go walking together with the children—it's the best exercise there is.

Eating together is absolutely crucial. I want to say just a word about "the curse of the TV meal." I am extremely regretful that we had so many of our evening meals in the den in front of the television set. My wife and I were in the first generation of parents to have a television

2. For information about a family council, see Rudolf Dreikurs, *The Challenge of Child Training: A Parent's Guide* (New York: Hawthorn, 1972), pp. 57–62; and Rudolf Dreikurs and Vicki Soltz, *Children: The Challenge* (New York: Hawthorn, 1964), pp. 301–5.

set. We allowed it to control us rather than controlling it. There is something detrimental about allowing television programs to usurp family interaction at mealtime. With few exceptions, plan to spend your mealtimes around the table with the television turned off.

Another disruption at mealtime is different schedules, especially if husband and wife both work or one or the other travels a lot. It helps to discuss the problem, make a commitment to having a family meal around the table, and do the best you can with the interruptions of varying schedules, even if it means eating without one of the parents being present on certain days. Related to this is the problem of over-busyness. Some parents are simply too busy. Again, it comes down to a basic commitment that family mealtime takes top priority with few exceptions. As your children grow older, you will see the importance of conversation during mealtimes with the whole family. Moreover, this is also one of the best times for a family to pray together. If you don't pray together while the children are at home, it won't be long before it's too late—they will be gone.

There are those special days for family togetherness: Christmas, Thanksgiving, Mother's and Father's days, birthdays, Easter, other holidays. Make the most of these days. Another of my regrets is not making more of selected ritual on Christmas and Thanksgiving. These two religious holidays provide tremendous opportunity for religious teaching for the entire family. Develop your own brief ritual around the tree on Christmas or at the table on Thanksgiving. Read selected Bible passages, use candles (especially throughout December, Advent candles on the dining table are more appropriate on each Sunday leading up to Christmas Day), pray, and include a brief comment from those who wish to say something about "what this day means to me."

Worshiping together can be another vital part of family togetherness. The old-fashioned "family altar" is almost a thing of the past. I'm afraid television has taken its place. If you want your children to catch the spirit of your own relationship to God, however, there needs to be a regular time when parents and children read from the Bible and pray together. Each family will need to set its own best time, place, and method, but *do it!* You'll never regret it. Just remember that with small children, keep it short and simple and use a modern translation of the Bible (e.g., the Living Bible, the New International Version, the Good News Bible).

At Church

Some of the best friends and most meaningful relationships will be those you cultivate in a local congregation of fellow Christians. The old adage that "the church is full of hypocrites" is a myth and a poor excuse for those who really want to drop out anyhow. Obviously, every church has its complainers, critics, preacher-haters, grumblers, and negative examples. But what human organization doesn't? Every civic club, fraternal organization, sorority, community-improvement group, and political party has these types of people, but we don't let them get in the way of our meaningful participation in those groups, do we? Every hospital or clinic has its grumpy nurse or curt doctor, but if I need medical attention, I go for help.

The negative people, the so-called hypocrites, are really expressing their own personality problems by that kind of behavior. Their real problem is themselves. They may have a problem with God, also. I'm not about to let those people ruin my relationships with the overwhelming majority of wonderful and loving people I find in the church. Actually, I have found that the few unhappy, negative, and critical people who are in the church are people who were not discipled in the Christian life and are consequently immature in their faith. Moreover, they are generally unloved, and are craving attention and recognition (another form of love). If they bother me, then that's my problem. Such people need my love and acceptance, not my avoidance.

Within the life of the church there are several opportunities for developing relationships on level 5: serving on committees, participating in social fellowships, attending worship services and *participating* actively therein, engaging in Bible study and other types of classes, sharing in witnessing groups, participating in prayer-and-share groups or mission-action groups, being involved in retreats with small groups, and engaging in recreational activities sponsored by the church. In these activities you can develop some of the most significant friendships you'll ever have. Here is where I found my wife, my very best friend today.

With Your Peers

As I discuss level 5, the social-interaction level, I have not intentionally overlooked the large number of single adults, including both the never-married and the formerly-married. This is a sizable group in our society today, larger than ever. Also, I am not overlooking the fact that some of your closest friends are not to be found in marriage and the family but will be your peers, those within your age group at school, at work, in the church, and in the community at large.

As a matter of fact, everyone needs friends of both sexes who are peers. Your spouse and children cannot meet all of your needs nor should they, with one exception: your total sexual needs ought to be met by your spouse. There are five categories of basic human needs: mental, social, emotional, physical, and spiritual. To expect one person to meet all of your needs is to overload his or her circuits. We each need a cluster of close friends from among our peers.

At school you can be a part of a study group, a debate or sports team, or a music or drama group. At work, you may be able to be a part of a task group, a think tank, or an ad hoc committee on special assignment. In the church, there are several possibilities that I've already mentioned. In the community, you may be a member of the city council, a civic club, or a community-improvement league where you can work with your peers in accomplishing constructive tasks. Such involvements also help to pull you out of your personal shell or religious ghetto into the wider community where your talents and time are needed.

The Strength of Interaction

Doing things with other people provides a unique kind of strength for deepening relationships.

Being human requires interaction. Humans are social beings and, therefore, require the strength gained from social interaction. I cannot exist for long in a social vacuum. While writing this book here at Oxford, I have been away from my wife for several weeks. Needless to say, I have had to struggle with loneliness. Writing itself is a very lonely work. One has to be alone for several hours to get anything written. Most all of my contacts here have been on a conversational level, which has its limitations. It has helped a great deal for my older son, Nelson, to join me for about five weeks of my stay here. We have taken several short side trips to Stratford, Blenheim, Windsor, London, and surrounding territory to see the sights together. We eat together and go walking together. Our interaction has given me strength to keep writing.

Social interaction is vital to healthy human living. Studies show

that it really is important to your health. Sustained isolation or loneliness can be very detrimental to one's mental and physical health.
Without others we become weak. In American society we tend to ig-
nore this truth and thus neglect our health.

There is a line in an old wedding ceremony about how in marriage
"joys are doubled and sorrows are halved." That certainly applies to
social interaction also. Doing things together on a sustained basis
brings the strength of doubling your joys and pleasures while also
reducing the impact of sorrow, loss, and disappointment.

I once got a major job promotion involving higher rank and salary
(not to speak of the prestige it brought). I called home and told my
wife. She rejoiced with me, but I was overwhelmed when I drove into
the driveway at the end of the day. She and the children had prepared
and hung over the entrance to the garage a large banner that read,
"Welcome Home Conquering Hero." That could never have happened
without them. It made me a stronger person that day.

In my last pastorate at Los Alamos, the deacons and I (and our
wives) came to be a very close-knit team leading the church there to
become one of the finest, most creative, most innovative, and fastest-
growing congregations in New Mexico. In five years our leadership
teamwork resulted in a growth in attendance from around eighty to
more than three hundred on Sundays. New facilities were built. A
vibrant small-group support system involved more than 75 percent of
the adults on a weekly basis. Our evangelism ministry reached many
new families and individuals. An aggressive discipling program was
started. The joy of seeing this happen was equally shared by these lay
leaders, but the joy was doubled because we worked together. Words
fail me in trying to describe the personal strength gained in such an
experience.

Sorrows are also halved in doing things together as a group. A loss
or a grief is much easier to bear when it is being shared with friends.
There is great strength in such comfort from those with whom you are
associated in common activities.

Mutual support is a kind of therapy. Jess Lair has subtitled one of
his books *Mutual Need Therapy*.[3] Lair contends, in his own unique
style, that there is a sort of therapeutic by-product in two or more
people being interdependent. In our prayer-and-share groups in Los

3. Jess Lair, *I Ain't Well, But I Sure Am Better: Mutual Need Therapy* (New York:
Doubleday, 1975).

Alamos, I saw several people pull out of depression, gain new purpose for living, experience growth as a parent dealing with serious parent-child conflict, come to grips with suicidal tendencies, overcome feelings of despair in a marriage grown stale, rediscover faith through prayer, or gain the will to ask someone for forgiveness for an old wrong. My list of illustrations of healing would be almost endless.

The strength of a group is almost mystical. It is so much more than the sum of the strength of its individual members. A group in action becomes almost a personality in itself. One of our support groups in Los Alamos once reached out to a man who had attempted suicide. The gun had failed to fire just as his next-door neighbor, one of our deacons, ran into his house to try to stop him. The man's former wife had called from another state after he had called her to tell her what he was about to do. I got involved from the personal-counseling angle, but when this man joined one of our groups, he found a new source of strength. The group became a kind of new family for him. The man has since remarried and has his life in order again.

Moreover, the social part of you develops when you engage in action with others. Several lives can become intertwined as people engage in a common endeavor. There is really no such thing as a single, unrelated *individual*. I am actually a cluster of social roles that tie me to several persons. My roles have included father, husband, son, brother, uncle, cousin, brother-in-law, son-in-law, pastor, teacher, friend, neighbor, stranger, taxpayer, citizen, voter, customer, and counselor. In the context of doing things with others, either as a couple or in a small group, the social dimension of my personality develops, and I become a person of stronger ego because of the shared strength of others who relate to me.

The strength of interaction with others is also seen when people share tasks to accomplish common goals that otherwise could not be met. Obviously you could never, by yourself, know the joys, the sense of achievement, and the reaching of goals that are to be found in a family. There are some things you can never do alone.

Members of one of our prayer-and-share support groups in Los Alamos decided after several months to get their minds off of themselves and take on a common project of rendering whatever support was needed to the Baptist Indian Center in Santa Fe. The Indian missionary made several suggestions, and the group went to work: repainting the building, repairing the plumbing and wiring, remodeling the kitchen, stocking the pantry shelves and storeroom with food, and furnishing several types of literature and Bibles for classes. As individuals these people could not and would not have done this, but as a group interacting together on mission they did a superb job.

When people relate together as a team, a family, a group, a church, or even a couple and accomplish something worthwhile (e.g., a family gets their three children through college, a team wins a game, a group feeds several hungry people and gives new hope to a community, a church builds a new sanctuary for worship and increases its missionary giving simultaneously, a couple has a new baby) there is an esprit de corps, a sort of psychological and spiritual adrenalin that flows through their lives. The thrill of common achievement injects a quality of strength that encourages further goal setting and pursuing. "Nothing succeeds quite like success." And certain kinds of success are possible only in and through groups.

The Strains of Confrontation

The social-interaction level not only can provide a positive experience of achievement and growth but also can bring about the strains of confrontation. Anytime two or more people try to do anything together, there is always the possibility of conflict.

Interaction produces conflict. If you lived alone and never saw anyone else, there would never be any conflict. The old saying, "It takes two to tango," applies here as well. I know more about conflict in marriage and family and in my work than anywhere else. If both husband and wife are headstrong and dogmatic, conflict is assured. Carole and I have had differences of opinion on several crucial matters, primarily finances, relatives, and sex. We have also had disagreements over methods and goals. We have always agreed on the importance of serving God, but not on how to do that. Early in our marriage she believed that serving God in a small inconspicuous church was probably more spiritual than serving Him in a large and well-known church. Of course, I wanted to serve Him in a large, prestigious (and well-paying!) congregation. She could sound very pious in explaining her reasons. So could I with mine.

The truth of the matter was that neither of us understood our motives for setting different goals for our lives. In time we discovered that what she really wanted was to avoid the constant spotlight and growing demands and expectations placed upon the wife of the pastor of a large church. Naturally, she wanted the income of the large pastorate but not the pressures. My motive was pure and simple: ego. The larger the church, the more important I would be. The salary would also be a monthly reminder of that importance. My culture and denomination encouraged me indirectly at this point by constantly rewarding the pastors of the larger churches with more recognition than pastors of the smaller ones. Unfortunately, this is still going on in just about every denomination.

I've also seen more than my share of conflict in the church. Usually this has been due to immature people jockeying for recognition and power. They also felt neglected by the pastor. Again, differences of opinion and disagreements over methods and goals become the ingredients for confrontation. Both sides often use anger to intimidate the other side. "If you insist on having your way in this matter, it will split the church." This means that the one making the statement will do his or her part in causing the split. One thing leads to another, and before you know it, a verbal and emotional battle is under way.

Three things I have learned about conflict. Conflict is normal; it is a part of human experience. Conflict is inevitable; it is going to happen at some time, so expect it and don't be surprised when it comes. Conflict is resolvable; there is a solution and a way to handle it that can be the means for growth. Later in this chapter I will recommend a method for resolving conflict.

When conflict develops out of open confrontation in your marriage, with your children, at church, or with your friends across the fence or at work, there are four possible reactions or steps you can choose. One, you can revert to shallower levels of relating, probably level 1, avoidance. Just pull out and retreat to your own position or to those who agree with you. Many a wife has threatened to go home to mother (I've always wondered why father isn't mentioned in those threats). Many a husband has decided to take up with his secretary or another woman at work. Many couples just pull back and pout for a few days or weeks.

Two, you can try to discover the nature of the problem. You can calm down, back off from a conflict stance, stop making threats, and use your common sense to assess the reasons for the conflict. Calm conversation at this point can help, especially if you'll use "I messages" instead of "you messages".[4] For example, you might say, "I really think

4. Thomas Gordon, *Parent Effectiveness Training: The Tested New Way to Raise Responsible Children* (New York: Peter H. Wyden, 1970), pp. 115–38, gives an especially helpful explanation of these two approaches in conversation.

I have been overstating my position and that I am being motivated to achieve the right goals with the wrong means. I'm really upset by all this conflict, and when I can get my anger under control I can be more reasonable" (I messages); rather than, "You stupid idiot, don't you know that if you had even the brain of a flea you could see that I'm right after all; you're the cause of our conflict because you are so self-ish and egotistical; this whole mess is your fault; now you listen to me . . ." (you messages).

Moreover, if you'll give one another a chance, you might discover that one has a physical problem (a woman's menstrual cycle is often a big part of marital conflicts) or an emotional problem (grief over the loss of a parent or one's job). One has a financial problem (not enough money to pay all the bills), and another has recently lost face in a social situation (didn't make the team at school, or was by-passed for a promotion). The immediate conflict is often the symptom of a deeper disturbance that is not always apparent.

Three, you can utilize the open lines of communication. There is no easy trick to this. Thomas Gordon's suggestions for "active listening" are a useful approach to learn.[5] You can open lines of communication by backing away from an aggressive and argumentative stance, kindly expressing your feelings while inviting the other or others to do like-wise, reflecting what you're hearing in friendly and fresh language to see if you really understand, and carefully using touching to communicate your concern for the other. Finally, go for help if the situation appears to be beyond your ability to cope. A friendly, understanding, fair, and disinterested person may be able to bring clarity and sanity to the situation.

Most conflict resolution moves through eight stages:

1. Contention (something produces strife)
2. Condemnation (accusations are made)
3. Confusion (participants are at a loss to know what to do)
4. Confrontation (someone recommends that we sit down and look things over)
5. Consideration (each considers the other's views)
6. Communication (feelings, viewpoints, and goals are freely shared)
7. Conciliation (mutual concessions and compromises are made)
8. Cooperation (agreement to work together in spite of differences and the past)

5. Ibid., pp. 49–94.

Since these all start with the letter *C,* maybe you can remember them easily in the heat of conflict! Analyze any conflict and see how this process works. Not all conflict will be resolved. It must be a give-and-take situation if there is to be resolution. But all conflict is resolvable if all parties are willing and committed to finding a way.

The Theology in a Preposition

In the New Testament there is an amazing preposition that is found many times either alone in a prepositional phrase or as a prepositional prefix attached to a noun or verb. It is the Greek word *sun,* which can be translated "along with, in company with, together with," or simply "with." This is the great relational preposition of the New Testament. It is used 123 times by itself in a prepositional phrase. As a prepositional prefix connected to almost one hundred different words, it is used countless times throughout the New Testament.

Just a few examples will suffice to show how this significant little relational preposition or prefix is used in the Scriptures. The early Christians are described as believing together (Acts 2:44), ministering together (Acts 2:45), worshiping together (Acts 2:46), growing together (Acts 2:47), rejoicing and weeping together (Rom. 12:15). They are described as fellow heirs, members, and partakers (Eph. 3:6), fellow comprehenders (Eph. 3:18), fellow citizens (Eph. 2:19), fellow workers (1 Cor. 3:9; Phil. 4:3), fellow soldiers (Phil. 2:25), and yokefellows (Phil. 4:3).

Without question, the early church believed and practiced a relational theology.[6] Christians have died with, been buried with, and been raised with Christ (Rom. 6:4–11). Likewise, believers consider themselves members of God's new nation and family (Eph. 2:19), serving their Lord in a company of the committed (Acts 2:43–47). Strict isolationism and rigid individualism were utterly foreign to the New Testament churches. The social-interaction level was a vital part of the relationships of God's people in those early days. It should be no different today.

6. For a popular treatment of relational theology, see Bruce Larson, *The Relational Revolution* (Waco, TX: Word, 1976).

7

The Big Question: Is That All There Is?

This chapter will be a brief interlude between our discussion of levels 1–5 and levels 6–8. Level 5 is a crucial level because that's where most people stop and fail to go deeper. After a period of time at level 5, however, some people (myself included, a few years ago) finally get around to asking the big question: Is that all there is? In other words, is that as deep as one can go? Can't there be more to relationships than just doing things together?

Being Locked into the Social-interaction Level

In most every area of life—marriage, family, work, church, friends, and community—most people I have known have been locked into the social-interaction level of relating. They have rarely gone any deeper with anyone. Many have probably not been aware that there are deeper levels.

It is truly sad that most people, as they search for meaningful and close relationships, end up going only part way toward the deepest levels. They tend to stop at level 5. Why? It is for highly individual reasons. Some may not be aware that there are deeper levels and therefore never seek what they do not know exists. One of the primary purposes of this book is to reveal the existence and possibilities of the deeper levels. People do not dig for treasure that they do not know exists. Others have seen, or possibly experienced in a fleeting moment, the deeper levels as expressed by friends, but were frightened by the closeness. They were too heavily conditioned by the distance factors in their culture to drum up the courage to go deeper. I believe the majority remain at level 5 because, as it seems, everyone else is doing it.

Keep in mind that I am not suggesting that you should try to develop deeper relationships with everyone. Most of our relationships at work, in the church, and in the community will retain a degree of distancing. This is to be expected. It is even healthy. My concern at this point, however, is that we usually go no deeper than level 5 with *anyone*.

Other reasons for remaining at the social-interaction level might include the belief that we experience adequate friendship at level 5. After all, isn't it friendship for us to enjoy doing the same things together? We mustn't forget George Eliot's reminder: "Friendships begin with liking or gratitude—roots that can be pulled up."[1] I don't know how many books on marriage I have read which suggest directly or indirectly that a meaningful marriage is one in which the couple enjoys living at what amounts to level 5. Few authors seem to be aware that there's anything more.

In addition, I believe that our overly active urban society drives people to achieve their maximum in a career, to make as much money as possible in order to buy all the things they're supposed to own to prove that they're successful, and to work hard enough to prove that they have worth as persons. This last point comes out of what is called the Protestant work ethic, which among other things stresses that you are worth only what you *do*, rather than that you have worth as a human being. Consequently, most people today are simply too busy to go any deeper than level 5. Developing friendships at the deeper levels requires time, which these folks do not believe they can spare.

In my case I got locked into level 5 because, as I suggested earlier, no one ever told me there's more. When Carole and I married, we had almost no idea what we were getting into so far as a deep relationship was concerned. Typically, our parents never talked to us about such things. I doubt if they ever went past level 5 themselves, with a few

1. George Eliot, *Daniel Deronda*, bk. 4, chap. 32.

fleeting exceptions on the caring level. They certainly never let on if they did reach sharing and intimacy. Our public-school teachers never told us about the deeper levels. Our Sunday-school teachers certainly never did. Our friends obviously knew nothing about depth. So we stumbled into the dark together and by the grace of God have survived to find that there is something more.

In more recent years, after discovering levels 6, 7, and 8, I began to look at the typical church situation (whatever "typical" is) and realized that the church isn't always programed to foster relationships on deeper levels. Occasionally you may find a church where level 6 is approached by some of the more sensitive members whose caring spirit is obvious to all. Even then it may be a rather broadcast kind of caring that "loves everybody" and wants to "win the whole world to Jesus" but never gets around to dealing in a one-on-one caring relationship. A friend of mine who now pastors a large church in the Deep South once told me that a well-known former pastor of the church he serves "loved the whole world but couldn't stand people!" There's too much of that in all of us.

Further, church activities tend to be functionally goal-oriented toward bigness. The bigger the Bible class the better. In Texas we are especially aware of the great theological "truth" that "big is better," except that no one can seem to find any biblical foundation for it. It surely isn't a heresy, is it?

Sunday-school classes are not structured for closeness: time is too short (only forty-five minutes once a week), most teachers lecture the members who sit and passively listen, many classrooms are not arranged to allow for expressing closeness, and in many churches the classes are entirely too large (25–100 members). Actually, any group with more than 10–12 members is too large for developing *depth* between the members. If any achieve depth, it is in spite of, not because of, the organization of the class.

Church committee work is too business- and activity-oriented for depth to be reached. Public worship services in the auditorium or sanctuary do not encourage closeness. The services tend to be almost solely one-way communication or are heavily entertainment-oriented for a passive audience. Most church activities will be conducted on levels 4 and 5. I contend that this is a basic reason why so many churches are in trouble: too many unhappy Christians who can't figure out what's wrong while they're doing all this great and wonderful church work that doesn't seem to produce the joy they're looking for.

They know they're supposed to love one another but few ever get around to it, it seems. I believe the distance factor is a large part of the reason for so many dropouts. When you have a few close friends in the church, you don't drop out, because you don't leave your friends! But friendships require closeness and depth.

I have already suggested in chapter 1 the problem of fear and in-security some people have at the thought of developing meaningful close relationships. It is a fact that a lot of people remain at level 5 because it's safer. There are fewer risks involved, such as running the risk of being rejected. "If people never see my innermost self, they'll never know me for the rascal I really am," some reason. Folks with a poor and negative self-image will likely feel this way.

The Problem of Relational Deficiency

There is a certain danger to be faced when people do not go any deeper than the social-interaction level. In time, a major problem develops which can ruin some good relationships. When a person does not go into the deeper levels of caring, sharing, and intimacy, a relational deficiency develops. This is expressed in one's becoming judgmental. A person tends to be overly critical of others or negative about life in general. This has been true in my own life. Because I was not close to anyone, I tended to be very negative. No one could please me. Nothing was right. Everything seemed wrong. I wrote off this kind of behavior as due to my "perfectionism." And it made everyone around me miserable.

A lot of pastors are this way because, after all, "they are not supposed to have any close friends in the church." The fact is that they are relationally starving to death. "Every pastor needs a pastor,"[2] but who will it be? Every pastor also needs some very close friends. If the pastor cannot or should not have any close friends in the church, then it stands to reason no one else should either. But we don't reason that way. We just go on being unfair to the pastor, keeping him at a distance, and relationally depriving him of deep psychological nutrition. All of this is in the name of keeping the pastor from playing favorites in the congregation.

A relationally deficient pastor behaves just like every relationally

2. See Louis McBurney, *Every Pastor Needs a Pastor* (Waco, TX: Word, 1977).

deficient person. He becomes judgmental, especially in the pulpit, and this in time rubs off on the congregation. Before long, controversy, conflict, or criticism is beyond control and the result is usually the dismissal of the pastor or the division of the church. All of this is so unnecessary.

You can easily see, I trust, what a relationally deficient husband or wife will do. It doesn't matter whether the criticism aimed at each other is accurate or not. You can tear any marriage to pieces if you want to do that. Imperfections are always there to criticize. But is that what we really want to do? Of course not. Then why do we do this to each other, after having pledged to love each other "until death do us part"? Relational deficiency is the reason.

Relational deficiency means that something very important is missing. That something is a cluster of resources to be found at the deeper levels. These resources are fundamentally emotional in nature. First, there is the feeling of support. Others are undergirding, strengthening, and encouraging you as a person of worth and significance. Likewise, you have the opportunity to provide support to others who are especially appreciative. Affirmation is being both given and received. When support is missing from our relationships, we feel the loss keenly.

Second, there is the feeling of being understood. You are open to others, and others are open to you. A mutual trust develops. There is great comfort in knowing that at least one other person understands your feelings and deepest needs. Likewise, you have the opportunity to understand another and to communicate that you do with full empathy and concern. A reciprocating trust is expressed between you and another. When compassionate understanding is missing, we feel the lack deeply. It is an uneasy and lonely feeling.

Third, there is the feeling of intimacy or closeness. This cannot be explained fully, only experienced. It is a feeling of oneness, unity, togetherness, of being cared for, loved, wanted, respected, esteemed, treasured, and even extolled—all wrapped up in one emotional relationship. It's something of that feeling you have when you walk into a room full of people and a close friend's face lights up upon seeing you. You have the opportunity to reciprocate. This feeling is always *mutual*. When intimacy is missing from your life, you feel uncomfortably, maybe painfully, incomplete.

Another danger of going no deeper than level 5 is that an ethical dynamic will likely be absent as a result of the missing resources.

Christian morality needs both content (teachings about right behavior) and motivation (the desire to do what is right). The Bible teaches that the indwelling Holy Spirit provides the Christian the ability to do the right (Rom. 8:1–11), but the Spirit usually provides that power in and through relationships at the deeper levels. In Romans 8, Paul refers to the Holy Spirit working in the hearts of believers. Notice how many of the words referring to believers are in the plural. The Spirit works through the collective body of the church and not isolated individuals only.

A passage that substantiates this view is Romans 5:1–5 (NIV).

> Therefore, since we have been justified through faith, we have peace with God through our Lord Jesus Christ, through whom we have gained access by faith into this grace in which we now stand. And we rejoice in the hope of the glory of God. Not only so, but we also rejoice in our sufferings, because we know that suffering produces perseverance; perseverance, character; and character, hope. And hope does not disappoint us, because God has poured out his love into our hearts by the Holy Spirit, whom he has given us.

Notice here that Paul stresses the work of the Spirit in "us" (plural, not singular). Also notice his reference to character (v. 4) and how "God has poured out his love into our hearts by the Holy Spirit" (v. 5). Paul's emphasis upon the plural rather than the singular stresses, to my way of thinking, the importance of relationships in Christian morality.

Moreover, Paul conceived of the church as a unified body, members who are in close relationships, just as the parts of a physical body are many yet closely bound together (Rom. 12:4–5). Paul rarely talks about ethics without placing his discussion in the context of close interpersonal relationships. Notice Romans 12:9–13 (NIV).

> Love must be sincere. Hate what is evil; cling to what is good. Be devoted to one another in brotherly love. Honor one another above yourselves. Never be lacking in zeal, but keep your spiritual fervor, serving the Lord. Be joyful in hope, patient in affliction, faithful in prayer. Share with God's people who are in need. Practice hospitality.

Apart from the resources found in the close relationships at the deeper levels, Christians will find little if any impetus for ethical living, especially over the long haul and under sustained stress.

I am not suggesting that Paul or any of the New Testament writers used terminology comparable to mine, nor am I saying that only on the levels of caring, sharing, and intimacy can a Christian ever find strength to do what is right, but I do believe that Paul and the other writers would substantially agree with my basic thesis: the importance of the deeper levels to ethics. Paul discusses relationships in anything but cool, distant, impersonal, and rationalistic terms.

Finally, confrontation, as discussed earlier in terms of conflict and strife, is usually a signal of the need to develop deeper relationships. Conflict is not always bad.[3] It can be the means to motivate two or more people to re-examine and deepen their relationship. When people have an argument over something, they're not indifferent. An argument can be an expression of love: "Let's go deeper."

Risking the Deeper Levels of Trust

At some point, you probably will make a decision to go beyond the social-interaction level and to risk the deeper levels of trust. You can do things with others without a great deal of trust because you aren't usually revealing a lot about yourself on level 5. To go deeper requires trust and that calls for risk. Trusting involves the risks of rejection and disappointment.

When I ran out of steam on level 5, I had the good fortune of being able to discuss my frustrations with some friends who I soon discovered were either in the same predicament as I or had gone deeper and found something better. I soon concluded, "Yes, there is more." My wife concurred, and together we launched out into the unknown (for us) territory of trusting our selves to each other and to a few others. Because God works in our relationships, this was also a way to trust God.

Not long into our experiment in trust, I read two books that gave me the idea of levels. One was by John Powell. He discussed five levels of communication. His numbers are reversed from mine, although they indicate the shallowest to the deepest, as mine do:

3. For excellent treatment of the subject of conflict in the church, see Daniel G. Bagby, *Understanding Anger in the Church* (Nashville: Broadman, 1979), and John Wallace, *Control in Conflict* (Nashville: Broadman, 1983). On conflict in marriage, see George R. Bach and Peter Wyden, *The Intimate Enemy: How to Fight Fair in Love and Marriage* (New York: Avon, 1981).

Level 5: cliché conversation

Level 4: reporting the facts about others

Level 3: my ideas and judgments

Level 2: my feelings (emotions); "gut level"

Level 1: peak communications

Powell sets forth his rules for "gut-level" communication (pp. 62ff.). At this point, he contrasts judgments and feelings:

Judgment	Some possible emotional reactions
I think you are intelligent	. . . and I am jealous.
	. . . and I feel frustrated.
	. . . and I feel proud to be your friend.
	. . . and it makes me ill at ease with you.
	. . . and I feel suspicious of you.
	. . . and I feel inferior to you.
	. . . and I feel impelled to imitate you.
	. . . and I feel like running away from you.
	. . . and I feel the desire to humiliate you.

Furthermore, he defines level 1 as "a complete emotional and personal communion." This level is occasional, never continual, and is similar to what Abraham Maslow called peak experiences.[4]

I had some problems with Powell's list, although I appreciated his treatment. He didn't cover all the bases of my experience. Moreover, his treatment of each level was too individualistic, not taking into consideration the relational dimension. Also, I felt that the term *communication* did not adequately describe the full range of relationships: behavior, attitudes, values, as well as the content of what one says or thinks.

Another book that helped me was by Jess Lair.[5] He identified four levels of relationships:

___

4. John Powell, *Why Am I Afraid to Tell You Who I Am?* (Niles, IL: Argus Communications, 1969), pp. 50ff.
5. Jess Lair, *I Ain't Well, But I Sure Am Better: Mutual Need Therapy* (New York: Doubleday, 1975), pp. 70–72. See also Jerry White and Mary White, *Friends and Friendship: The Secrets of Drawing Closer* (Colorado Springs, CO: Navpress, 1982), who discuss three levels.

The lowest level: the people I can't stand

The minimum level, which we owe to everybody: courtesy and respect

The third level: complete acceptance

The fourth and highest level: where you are valued as you are

As you can see, Lair reverses the order of numbering because he does not use the metaphor of depth but of height as the most desirable level. His list has some of the same limitations as Powell's, and his distinction between the third and fourth levels is not as clear as it should be. The highest level is "when a person's face lights up when they see us," but that could mean different things to different people. At least Lair led me to think further about relationships.

With whom do you begin when seeking deeper relationships? Start at home if at all possible. You have the most to gain there. Begin with your spouse. I started with my wife. She had actually started sooner than I with a small group of women who, on the surface of things, had almost nothing in common: different ages, marital status, ages of children, and backgrounds. They started meeting as a prayer group but soon developed into a sharing group expressing a deep care for one another. Before long I could tell a distinct difference in Carole and began to ask the reasons. Her sharing with me what was happening to her began our journey together into a deep friendship.

There may be no way for you to involve your spouse: unwillingness, death, or divorce, as the case may be. Then look to the other members of your family: a sister or brother, mother or father, an aunt or uncle. Perhaps you can confide in your children, although this depends on their ages. At this point, all I'm talking about is an invitation to a deeper friendship.

In addition, look within your church. Here the likeliest prospects will be found. It's amazing how many people in the church are simply waiting to be invited to go deeper in relating. When I began my pastorate in Los Alamos in 1975, I proposed to the church leadership that we institute a system of small support groups. They were more than eager to try it. We began with the deacons and their wives for four months, after which we opened the program to the entire membership. Groups were to be led by the deacons, who had by then experienced what we were proposing. An amazing 75 percent of the adults responded, and we were able to maintain that percentage over the next five years as the church grew much larger.

Essentially, then, you look for people who feel the same need and are willing to run the same risks that you are. I doubt if you will find not one interested person. Quite the contrary, there are many looking for what you're looking for.

If you're going to get off dead center, then you'll have to make a commitment to go deeper. This decision will involve a willingness to risk and a willingness to trust. But, believe me, it's worth it.

The Number of People Grows Smaller

As I stated before, as you go deeper in relationships, the number of people to whom you relate will grow smaller on each level.

It is quite normal for one's closest and deepest friends to be fewer in number than those one relates to in more casual ways. Actually, I have observed that as one moves from level 1 on through level 8 the number of people decreases as one goes deeper. This is, after all, necessary. Close relationships require concentration of attention and a greater commitment of time for each person you relate to. I found that I simply do not have the time and opportunity to relate to very many people on the deeper levels. As time goes by and due to uncontrollable circumstances, some of the people I relate to on the deeper levels move out of the picture of my life and need to be and probably will be replaced by others.

One calculation of my own relationships in the recent past is this:

Level 1 (avoidance, positive and negative): thousands

Level 2 (greeting): hundreds

Level 3 (separate interests): fifty to seventy-five

Level 4 (common interests): thirty

Level 5 (social interaction): twenty

Level 6 (caring): twelve

Level 7 (sharing): five or six

Level 8 (intimacy): three

These are rough estimates except for the last three levels, where I can be very specific. I am not suggesting that this is average or typical or even desirable, only that these are approximate proportions for me at this time in my life. If I kept a daily diary I could be more specific about most of the levels; yet this would vary with the month of the year, where I was that month, and what I was doing during that time. The last three levels tend to be more fixed and definite as to the specific persons involved.

Moreover, intensity, which increases as you go deeper, imposes certain limitations in relationships. That is to say, the more intense you become in relating, the fewer people you will have time and energy for.

I ask the big question again: "Is that all there is?" The answer is *no*. There is more. Related questions that need to be asked are, "Am I locked into the social-interaction level?" If so, "Why? Am I aware of the danger of going no deeper? Am I willing to make the commitment to the deeper levels of trust? Can I identify a few people around me with whom I could start? When would I like to start? How can I do so?" In the remainder of this book we will look at the deeper levels. A decision to develop deeper relationships could be a turning point in your life, as it was for Carole and me.

8

Caring Enough to Get Involved

From here on we deal with the most meaningful levels of relating. Level 6 is the caring level. It is that level where you are communicating to a person: "You have my undivided attention. What can I do for you that you cannot very likely do for yourself? I care enough to get involved in meeting certain needs in your life." I don't mean for this message to sound paternalistic; in this chapter I am trying to convey the idea that what I can do that's good for you is also good for me. Remember, we need each other. Caring is a double blessing.[1]

Awareness and Sensibility

Two very important terms in our language are "awareness" and "sensibility." To function on the caring level calls for an understanding of the meaning of these words. Awareness is the condition of being conscious, not ignorant, having knowledge of something; well-informed. Sensibility is the capacity to feel, or exceptional openness to emotional impressions; delicacy of feeling, susceptibility, sensitivity.

As we move into the caring level, we are shifting away from *self*-centeredness to *others*-centeredness. We are becoming more conscious

1. For an excellent book about developing a caring ministry in a local church, refer to C. W. Brister, *Take Care: Translating Christ's Love into a Caring Ministry* (Nashville: Broadman, 1979).

114

of and informed about others around us. Becoming knowledgeable about others encompasses a wide range of information, but I am particularly thinking of other's needs, feelings, problems, hardships, and frustrations. Awareness of others requires that we take our eyes off of ourselves long enough to see others as they really are.

Caring also requires that we develop the capacity to feel and an openness to the emotional impressions that the needs of others can arouse within us. Instead of feeling self-pity over our own unmet needs, we feel a concern for others who are struggling to cope with life.

Therefore, the caring level calls me to move away from an obsession with myself, a sort of preoccupation with my own little world, to an awareness of the needs of others plus a sensitivity to this knowledge that moves me to do whatever I can about those needs. To use a couple of helpful metaphors, awareness requires an inner kind of radar to detect where others are in their life situations, whereas sensibility demands the growth and development of a lot of psychological and relational neurons within us.

We often hear it said that everyone has problems. No one questions this. The question we might debate is, what do you do about other people's problems? We all need problems to solve if we are ever to grow. A child has to learn to tie his or her shoelaces for him or herself eventually. To do it for him or her all the time is to rob the child of self-confidence, not to speak of creating embarrassing situations when school starts. So there is the beneficial element in human struggle. But what about the problems people can't handle alone?

There are right now people within your circle of relationships who have serious problems, in some cases so serious that they are contemplating self-destruction. Death for some looks better than life. You may not be aware of these problems or the seriousness of them. Some folks are pretty good at covering up and pretending all is well.

What if one person you know and see regularly is on the verge of a divorce, suffering from uncontrollable phobias, has just been told that his wife has a malignant tumor, has just been fired from his or her job, learned last week that her husband is having an affair with another woman, or last night discovered illegal drugs in her son's bedroom? The possibilities could be endless. If any of your friends is facing one of these problems, how likely are you to be aware of the situation, and what would you do if you knew? The point is, for most of us, there are people who need us.

Being aware of and sensitive to the needs of others is not always a simple or easy matter. Some people will not seem to want you to know about or get involved in their problems. They have been culturally conditioned to believe that they ought to handle their own problems. This is not all bad. We all need to learn to tie our own shoelaces. For example, no one else can solve a person's marital problems for him. However, there are those situations that folks simply cannot handle or cope with alone. In those cases, I need to be available and ready to help. This gives me, for one thing, a sense of mission and purpose. I needn't be pushy, but I do need to be available.

Reaching the caring level gives me this sense of mission and purpose. One of the things I enjoyed about being a pastor was the opportunity to help people who seemed overwhelmed in their life situations. Being a part of saving a marriage is an exhilarating and rewarding experience. Playing a role in helping two parents to rebuild a close relationship with a wayward son is extremely rewarding. People in the helping professions know the joyful sense of mission and purpose. This is one reason why they are often willing to work in positions where the salary is less than they could make in other types of work.

I have discovered that possessing awareness and sensibility is a vital part of being alive. One of the most pathetic situations I can think of is living life day by day and rarely if ever knowing what is going on in the lives of others and, if perchance an awareness of someone's needs did come to my attention, not feeling any concern.

You may have heard of the political candidate who was decrying the two major evils of society today: ignorance and apathy. When a voter asked him what he thought about unemployment and poverty, the candidate responded, "I don't know and I don't care."

There was a fine woman in one of my pastorates who was as devout and moral as any person you could find. However, her family members often bemoaned the fact that she was oblivious to what was going on in the lives of her children. She was so caught up in her own feelings and needs that other people's problems passed her by. She was both religious and self-centered, not exactly a happy combination. She, therefore, was not known as "vibrantly alive." To truly be alive you have to be *aware* and you have to be able to *feel*.

Levels of Awareness

In *caring* about others, you have to be *aware* of them. But what does this mean? There are different qualities of awareness in that the focus of awareness may vary. I have observed six levels of awareness. Describing these is helpful in explaining the different ways of being aware of others. I will explain each level from the perspective of my supposed awareness of you. The "you" could be any person in my circle of relating.

The physical level: that you are. Obviously, I must, first of all, be aware *that* you are: your physical presence. This means I recognize that you exist, that you look a certain way, that you are physically identifiable. It would also involve an awareness of your physical condition, for example, well-fed or hungry, well-dressed or in rags, comfortably warm or miserably cold, healthy or sick, young or old, male or female. This would include your physical needs and abilities or resources.

Have you ever been in a crowd or at a party, and after a while you realized that no one was aware that you were even there? Middle children have a tendency to feel ignored or left out. Some wives, whose husbands are extremely involved in their work and gone a lot from home, feel overlooked. I remember one wife telling me in a counseling session that there were evenings at home when her husband was so transfixed before the television (in his usual after-dinner trance) that she had the compulsive urge to stand up and scream, "Hey George, look, it's me! I'm over here!" He was not even aware of his wife's presence.

To be fully aware that a person exists, you have to look at him or her. The eyes communicate one's awareness. I notice that the British rarely look at people as they meet each other on the streets. If they don't know you, they don't look at you. The eyes can communicate so much, especially caring.

Some time ago, Thornton Wilder wrote a moving play called *Our Town*. How can one forget the scene where little Emily dies? She goes to the cemetery and is told, "Emily, you can return home for one day in your life. Which day would you choose?" She replied, "Oh, I remember how happy I was on my twelfth birthday. I'd like to go back on my twelfth birthday." The people in the cemetery cry out, "Emily, don't do it. Don't do it, Emily."

But she goes anyhow. Emily wants to see her mama and her papa again. The scene changes, and she is home. Emily, a twelve-year-old in a beautiful dress and with pretty, bouncing curls, strides down the stairs.

But Mama is too busy making the birthday cake to stop long enough to look at Emily. Emily says, "Mama, look at me. I'm the birthday girl." And Mama says, "Fine, birthday girl. Sit down and have your breakfast." Emily says again, "Mama, look at me." But Mama keeps on cooking.

Papa comes in and he's so preoccupied with making money that he doesn't look. Brother comes in and he's so busy with his own interests that he doesn't look either.

The scene ends with Emily standing in the middle of the stage, saying, "Please somebody, just look at me. I don't need the cake or the money. Please look at me." Yet nobody looks, and she turns to her mama once more and says, "Please Mama?" But then she turns and says, "Take me away. I've forgotten what it was like to be human. Nobody looks at anybody. Nobody cares anymore, do they?"[2]

The status level: what you are. If I go beyond awareness of your physical presence, then I will become aware of what you are: your status in society. By status I mean the social labels you wear. You may be a female, middle class, a college graduate, holding a certain set of convictions, beliefs, and opinions that reflect a Protestant background. Or you could be a male, of the working class, a high-school graduate, a Roman Catholic in religion and morality, a Democrat in politics, and a member of a labor union.

Whatever your status, it poses certain opportunities or privileges, problems or barriers, freedoms or limitations for you, and I will be aware of those. Your status is your social rank, and it tells me what you are in such a way that it will determine how I will talk with you, what I will expect from you, what you will expect from me, and where our relationship might go.

The identity level: who you are. Going a little deeper, I may become aware of who you are. This is much more than knowing your name. This is psychological awareness of your self-image. In other words, I become aware of how you see yourself. You may see yourself as beautiful, ugly, or average. You may think of yourself as intelligent, stupid, or mediocre. You may feel lovable or unlovable, good or bad, dirty or clean, big or little, acceptable or unacceptable.

Your self-image determines the script by which you live out your

2. Adapted from Thornton Wilder, *Our Town* (New York: Coward McCann, 1938), pp. 113–28, by Leo Buscaglia in *Living, Loving, and Learning,* ed. Steven Short (New York: Fawcett Columbine, 1982), pp. 33–34.

role in life.[3] If your self-image is that of a loser, then you will prove that you are in all sorts of ways. Your behavior is the result of your life script. When I am aware of who you are, I will be aware of how you see yourself.

This level also includes an awareness of your social perception: how you imagine that others see you. This will be very close to your self-image. Yet there is a difference. I've known certain youth who thought their parents saw them as "no good" but were determined to prove otherwise. Yet the parents' perceived perception left some definite psychological scars, often a deep resentment.

Your relational needs will be rooted here in the identity level. People who feel unloved, unwanted, and rejected do so largely because of their self-image and their perception of others' evaluation of them. If I know who you are, I will be more likely to know what your relational needs and resources are.

Most people who have come to me for counseling through the years have been people with poor, negative self-images, who felt unloved and rejected by others, who saw themselves as losers who couldn't do anything right, and who were fumbling along through life because they believed that's what they deserved. Once I became aware of who they were (how they saw themselves), then I was able to guide them toward building a new self-image.

The experiential level: where you are. If I can learn more about you, I may become aware of where you are, the experiential dimension of your life. This refers to what is happening in your life; as we say, "where you are coming from." All kinds of things may be happening to you now or in recent weeks or months: death of a loved one, a divorce, loss of a job or a promotion, a chronic illness in the family, news of imminent and serious surgery, a child has run away from home, your husband has just left you, to mention a few negatives. On the other side, you may have just gotten engaged, had a new baby, found a new and better paying job, been made president of the company, bought a new house, inherited a fortune, or just become a Christian.

This level also involves a sort of emotional awareness; that is, how these recent experiences in your life make you feel: depressed or elated, positive or negative. At this level I will be aware of your emotional

3. See Claude M. Steiner, *Scripts People Live: Transactional Analysis of Life Scripts* (New York: Grove, 1974). Also see Eric Berne, *Games People Play* (New York: Ballantine, 1978), pp. 110ff., 201ff.

state and needs. This will require that I be able to listen to your feelings about what has been or is happening to you. To reach this level I will need to be aware of what is happening in your life now, what effect this is having upon you, what you are doing about it, and what, if anything, you might want me to do in support.

The religious level: why you are. At one step deeper I will become aware of your religious view of your existence in the world: why you are. *Why* is the big religious question for everyone. Telling me you are a Christian or an agnostic, a Baptist or a Catholic, a Moonie or a Mormon, doesn't really tell me the answer to this question. From my own point of view, your denominational preference tells me only of your general view of God as expressed in some historic creed or body of doctrine. It doesn't tell me much about *you* as a person. I will be honest: if you tell me you're either a Moonie or a Mormon, I will consider you either confused or terribly deceived, and in so doing will be reflecting my personal interpretation of the Bible and theological stance.

The religious level reveals your sense of purpose, direction, and meaning for life (or lack of such). We might call this a kind of spiritual awareness of your reason for being, your place in the world, your role in God's plan (or that of some "superior power," as some see it), your purpose for living, your life goal—all of this as perceived by you. If you haven't fully worked out all this for yourself (and who has?), then this level will show me where you are in the search for the whys of life.

What I can learn about you on this level will also tell me something of the spiritual needs you have: a deeper understanding of prayer, how to better understand the Bible, resolving some problems with the institutional church as a result of past negative experiences, or a deeper exercising of faith in God.

The communication level: what you are saying. On this level, and it is debatable as to which of the six is the deepest, I become aware of what you are saying. By this time, you are trying to communicate your inmost feelings to me. There are at least two types of communication: informational, emphasizing content, data, facts, viewpoints, and interpretation of facts; and emotional, emphasizing feelings chosen in response to information, events, or interpretations. On this level there is a need for sensitivity to both types. We need "ears to hear."

The communication level reveals how I can know you. I need to be able to hear what you are saying. Do you ever feel like shouting to your family or friends, "No one ever listens to me!" or "No one ever hears what I'm trying to say!" Many suicides leave notes saying no one would listen to them. I'm convinced that most alcoholics, drug addicts, and divorced people feel this way.

On this level I must concentrate on your words, how you use them, your nonverbal communications, and the way you feel about what you are saying. How do I do this? I'm really not sure it can be explained. This ability to listen may be more of an art or a gift than a learned ability. I would hope that both are involved: a gift and a skill to be developed. A good word here is empathy: that is, the power of fully comprehending the feelings of the person being considered. It is the ability to *feel* what the other person is experiencing and feeling.

I believe that the communication level can also reveal how you and I can bless one another. To bless is not only to approve but also to express confidence, to encourage, and to affirm. If I hear what you are saying and feeling, I will reflect this to you and this becomes a source of strength. You will probably reciprocate, because I am trying to say some things too, and I hope that you will be on the communication level with my words and feelings also. If you are, we will bless each other.

Therefore, if we are to care for others, we must be aware of them, but awareness involves several levels, each of which is important to the process of caring.

A man walked into my office one day. I had never seen him before. His clothes and physical appearance told me he was poor, transient, hungry, and in need of some kind of help. I could see that he was probably unemployed, friendless, without family, uneducated, and feeling resentful and bitter. I discovered that here was a man who thought very poorly of himself and was a failure in every sense socially. He was alone, had no car and no money, had slept the night before under a bridge, and was feeling very depressed. He hadn't had a decent meal in days.

This stranger from nowhere had dropped out of the middle-class and working-class rat race, as he called it. He saw very little reason for living and had no hope for the future, living only a day at a time. His main concern was surviving that day, although he wasn't sure why. He was saying all of this to me, but primarily he was saying, "Love me a little, care about me some, help me through today, and I'll move on." I tried to hear and help. I felt very inadequate. However, people like this have taught me the importance of awareness. Jesus was always aware. So should we be.

The Courage to Get Involved

Caring for another calls for personal involvement. However, getting involved in someone else's life situation can be very time-consuming, awkward, possibly unwanted, emotionally draining, and even expensive. Therefore, you may need a great deal of courage to get involved, at least to remain involved for long.

John 3:16 provides us with a possible model. A paraphrase of this well-known verse might be: "For God cared so much for everyone in the world (past, present, and future) that He became personally involved in solving the most serious problem of the human race by giving Himself in the person of His Son in the ultimate sacrifice of His life in order that whoever learned to trust Him with all they are and have should not lose everything they are and have but should come to possess an eternal and abundant life." Consequently, God's care is our model for involvement. The paraphrase of another verse is even more succinct: "We care because God first cared for us" (1 John 4:19).[4]

If caring doesn't lead to involvement, then it really isn't God's kind of caring. Another paraphrased verse speaks to this: "Friends, let's stop merely talking about caring and begin to be serious about it by getting directly involved" (1 John 3:18). Our hesitancy to get involved in other people's problems may reveal our lack of courage. This kind of courage can come only from knowing and walking with God personally. To paraphrase 1 John 4:8, "He who does not care does not know God; for God is caring."

To get involved in others' lives you have to care enough to go out of your way to be present when you're needed. The well-known television commercial, "Reach out and touch someone," hints at so much more than making a simple phone call. It suggests making yourself available to another person in need of you. It means being present if at all possible. You can't really touch someone via the telephone.

One of the most caring people I know is my wife's brother, Dan Griffin, pastor of the Cliff Temple Baptist Church in Dallas. He doesn't just care for the members of his church; he cares for anyone who needs him regardless of where he or she is or what time of day or night it is. Many times I have known him to travel many miles to be with

4. Paraphrases here are the author's own.

someone who needed him. He does this without any promise of reward or reimbursement for expenses. It would never occur to him to ask.

It doesn't take long for people to find out, from the way he reaches out to people in need, that Dan is a genuinely caring person. He faithfully visits his people (and others) in hospitals, nursing homes, and at home; he counsels numerous people for several hours each week in his office. When death takes a member of a family, Dan is probably at his best in caring. If at all possible, everything else takes second place and he goes to be with the family. It is, therefore, not surprising that people by the hundreds throng to hear this man on Sundays in his pulpit: he is constantly reaching out to people, and they, in response, reach out to him. His popular thirty-minute television program on Sunday mornings on a Dallas-Fort Worth network affiliate draws a similar response. Dan's caring example has spread throughout the metroplex to the extent that Cliff Temple is widely known as a genuinely caring church.

Many fascinating stories could be told about Dan's caring ability in the life of his church: for example, how one doctor in the church, James Boyd, found another physician, Robert Gehring, in his office after hours one day in a drug-induced stupor. He was near death. Jim asked Dan to help him. For several months Jim and Dan counseled with Bob, becoming truly a life-support system for him. It wasn't long until Bob became a Christian and told his life story publicly before the church. He told about years of drug abuse, divorce and family problems, hospitalizations, and suicide attempts. Not many physicians would "go public" about such things. Talk about courage!

Now others in the medical community in Dallas are being helped by these three men. Bob subsequently told his story on the Phil Donahue television show, and Bob and Dan will soon publish a book about Bob's life and what Jesus Christ did in making a new Bob Gehring.[5] Caring is contagious!

The courage to get involved requires not only your willingness to be present when needed but also your compassion and empathy. Having compassion means "to suffer with" someone who is hurting. Empathy is understanding another's dilemmas and feeling as he or she does. The Gospel writers indicate that Jesus was often moved with compassion when He found people in distress (e.g., Matt. 9:36; 14:14; 15:32). Caring for others certainly must begin in the emotions.

I believe that several things in our modern urban society have caused

5. Robert Gehring, M.D. with Don Griffin, *Doctor Addict* (Grand Rapids: Zondervan, forthcoming in 1984).

us to develop an unfeeling and callous attitude toward people who are suffering. Television programing is especially responsible in this regard. In a normal week's time, we will view many accounts about pain, hardship, problems, and distress. We get used to seeing these. Our sensitivity becomes dull. Our emotions are washed out. Fiction has been portrayed so realistically so often that in time the real seems like fiction.

Moreover, the media so overwhelm us with the news of so many suffering people (e.g., world hunger, the murder of six million Jews by the Nazis, hundreds dying in one plane crash, fifty thousand killed on the highways each year, millions could die in a nuclear holocaust) that we simply cannot handle the thought of massive suffering. So we choose not to feel anything, even the pain of one person next door. We are more likely to weep in a movie theater than in a real situation.

How do you recover the capacity to feel? I'm not sure, but I think it has to start with one person who needs me. My choice to get involved may, at first, be very rational. The feelings may come *after* I get involved, even if it's nothing more than experiencing the gratitude of the other person. I believe that with enough practice, compassion and empathy can become habits, especially if you have a personal relationship with God, the author of human emotions.

Caring will cost you. You might as well face it. You're not going to care without paying a price. Caring may involve material or financial assistance for the person in need. You have heard it said that if you really want to know what a person is like, you will have to examine his or her checkbook stubs. Think about the checks you have written during the past month. How many could be classified as expressions of caring?

I recently learned that one of my colleagues found one of our students and his family facing this past Christmas season with no place to live. The student had lost his job and could not pay the month's rent. Until he could find a new job, he and his family were going to have to move out of their apartment. My colleague got involved to the degree that he and his wife took this young family into their own home during the Christmas vacation, eventually found the student a less expensive apartment nearer the campus, paid the first month's rent, and helped him to find a new job. This man cared enough to give financially. He also cared enough to give encouragement and affirmation. Obviously, that student learned something from that professor that no lecture could ever teach.

However, we often overlook that many times this kind of support can be given without costing us one cent. There are a lot of depressed people who are financially well-off. Most of the depressed people I have counseled did not want or need money. They needed hope, something money cannot buy.

Some people need us to care enough to give ourselves: presence, time, and friendship. Most needy people don't want what we have. What they would like most is *us*. I have no idea what my best friends are worth, but these people are worth a lot to me as friends. Their friendship makes me rich!

A few years ago, Lewis Smedes, who teaches at Fuller Theological Seminary in California, learned that a friend of many years named Cal, who always lived at a great distance, had been diagnosed as having terminal cancer. Lewis immediately flew from California to Michigan to spend a few days visiting his friend. The airplane ticket, meals, and lodging must have been expensive for him, but he cared enough to give himself to Cal in his last days. On the last day of his visit, as he left Cal's hospital room, Cal said, "Lew, it's all right." A few days later Cal died, but I believe Lewis helped to make it possible for Cal to say, "It's all right." Smedes told the story for another reason, but I could not fail to see that here was someone who cared enough to give *himself* when needed.[6]

Your faith in God is something else you can care enough to give. It's stunning how many people in this world have *never* heard another person share with them their personal relationship with God. This is something you would naturally expect Christians to do. However, we are so afraid these days of being "personal." Why? If knowing God personally is the most important thing in all the world, as Christians claim, then we ought to be giving this knowledge away as often as possible. If you had an indisputable cure for cancer, would you keep it to yourself?

When I get involved in the lives of others and give myself to them, I am making an investment, the best investment of my life: in others. I have friends who think I will regret it some day, but I have never spent much time investing in property, stocks and bonds, or business ventures. I prefer to spend what time I have on earth investing in

6. Lewis Smedes, *How Can It Be All Right When Everything Is All Wrong?* (New York: Harper and Row, 1982), pp. 1–2.

people. Caring for people in need is one of these marvelous investments that pays high dividends for years to come.

Jesus talked about finding yourself by losing yourself "for my sake" (Matt. 10:39; 16:25). I do not believe it is violating the meaning of a text on discipleship to suggest that one way to find yourself is to lose yourself in others for Jesus' sake. Jesus was constantly investing Himself in others. This was how the early church started: Jesus so invested Himself in a handful of disciples that they, and those who were added later, took on His characteristics ("they took note that these men had been with Jesus," Acts 4:13, NIV) and later identified themselves as "the body of Christ" (1 Cor. 12:27, NIV).

As far as we know, Jesus never accumulated any money, owned any property, or invested in any sort of financial endeavor (see Matt. 8:20). He chose to invest in people, knowing the payoff would be eternal dividends far beyond the value of temporal wealth. He actually warned against laying up treasures on earth, because they don't really last (Matt. 6:19–21).

I have found tremendous satisfaction in seeing myself being reproduced or extended through the lives of those in whom I invested my time, energy, money, counsel, encouragement, and guidance. Caring for people in need is certainly one way to "cast your bread upon the waters," knowing that "after many days you will find it again" (Eccles. 11:1, NIV). Jesus was referring to the same principle when He said, "And if anyone gives a cup of cold water to one of those little ones because he is my disciple, I tell you the truth, he will certainly not lose his reward" (Matt. 10:42, NIV).

Biblical Patterns for Caring

The Bible is the story of a caring God. It is full of the images of caring. God's caring produces a community of caring. Therefore, it is important to reflect upon the biblical patterns.

From the very beginning, God is revealed as the creator and sustainer of all His creation (Gen. 1–2). Especially for man, God provided place, purpose, food, mate, and task. The earliest stories of Israel reveal God as the great Provider (Gen. 22:1–14, especially vv. 8 and 14). God always provides for His people (Deut. 11:8–17).

The Bible is full of the promises of God, which I view as His affirmations to us. These also reveal His caring heart. One of the most meaningful promises is in Philippians 4:19 (NIV), where Paul says, "And my God will meet all your needs according to his glorious riches in Christ Jesus." Another is from Peter, who says, "Humble yourselves, therefore, under God's mighty hand, that he may lift you up in due time. Cast all your anxiety on him because he cares for you" (1 Peter 5:6–7, NIV).

If you take almost any book in the Bible and read verse by verse, you can make a long list of God's promises. A quick look at the Book of Isaiah reveals God's promises of moral cleansing (1:18), safety (3:10; 43:1–3), forgiveness (6:7; 43:25; 55:6–7), a Savior (7:14; 11:1–3), peace (11:6–9), the Messiah (42:1–4; 52:13–53:12; 61:1–4), life (55:1–5), answer to prayer (58:6–9), and God's own presence (60:1–3), to list only a few.

I have already given a paraphrase of John 3:16, but I do want to re-emphasize that the greatest example of God's caring is the gift of His Son, Jesus Christ. It is possible to render the word normally translated in the Bible as "love" with the word *care*. "In this is caring, not that we cared for God but that He cared for us and sent His Son to be the sacrifice for our sins" (1 John 4:10; author's paraphrase, based on RSV). God's expression of caring is always personal. He didn't simply send a message of care, but sent His Son.

God's kind of caring is generally the unexpected kind: for the unlovely and needy. He expresses care for outsiders, outcasts, rejects, the despised, the ugly, undesirables, the sinful, the unclean. He shows concern for the hungry, thirsty, sick, dying, lonely, sorrowful, weak, young, old, poor, powerless, imprisoned, suffering. God always champions the cause of the downtrodden and needy. This is so obvious that biblical references here are unnecessary. Accounts of one or more of these situations can be found on almost any page of the Bible.

Throughout the Gospels we find numerous accounts of Jesus healing the sick, cleansing the lepers, accepting the outcasts, forgiving the immoral, raising the dead, comforting the grieving, and giving hope to the despairing. Everywhere Jesus went He reached out to people in need. He taught His followers to do the same.

The record of Acts and the letters of Paul and the other New Testament writers reveal that those who became followers of Jesus therefore sought to emulate His example of caring for people. First Thessalonians provides a beautiful illustration of this spirit in the early church: "Therefore encourage one another and build each other up, just as in fact you are doing. . . . And we urge you, brothers, warn those who are idle, encourage the timid, help the weak, be patient with everyone" (5:11, 14, NIV). The early Christians not only preached the way of salvation but also fed the hungry, healed the sick, comforted the sorrowing, accepted the social rejects, and encouraged the despairing. They cared for people in need, just as Jesus did. The church today should be no different in this regard.

Another major biblical pattern for caring is what I call the "one-another" religion of the early Christians. The Greek word translated "one another" is used approximately one hundred times in the New Testament. My count shows forty-two times in the Gospels and Acts, forty-one times in Paul's letters, and eighteen times in the other writings. This word describes something important in the church's lifestyle.

Paul's uses of this word illustrate what happens on the caring level.

1. Mutual devotion. "Be devoted to one another in brotherly love" (Rom. 12:10a, NIV).
2. Preferential respect. "Honor one another above yourselves" (Rom. 12:10b, NIV).
3. Affirmation and encouragement. "Therefore encourage one another and build each other up" (1 Thess. 5:11, NIV).
4. Unity. "May the God who gives endurance and encouragement give you a spirit of unity among yourselves [harmony with one another, RSV] as you follow Christ Jesus . . ." (Rom. 15:5, NIV).
5. Acceptance. "Accept one another, then, just as Christ accepted you, in order to bring praise to God" (Rom. 15:7, NIV).
6. Instruction. ". . . competent to instruct one another" (Rom. 15:14b, NIV).
7. Mutual service. ". . . serve one another in love" (Gal. 5:13b, NIV).
8. Mutual support. "Carry each other's burdens, and in this way you will fulfill the law of Christ" (Gal. 6:2, NIV).
9. Forgiveness and kindness. "Be kind and compassionate to one another, forgiving each other, just as in Christ God forgave you" (Eph. 4:32, NIV).
10. Mutual submission. "Submit to one another out of reverence for Christ" (Eph. 5:21, NIV).

It is quite clear to me that the early Christians had reached the caring level in their fellowship and that this was attractive to outsiders as well as a strong factor in retaining members. Caring can make the church great once again.

The story is told that when Sinclair Lewis, the famous American novelist, moved to a retirement home on the outskirts of Rome, an Italian reporter heard of it and got the idea of interviewing the famous author. The reporter made an appointment and drove out to Lewis's home to find him sitting in a rocking chair on the front porch.

The reporter reflected for a time with Lewis on the themes of his several novels: *Main Street,* which treated the problems of the narrowness of life among common people and the hollowness of a superficial intellectualism that despised the common people; *Babbitt,* which dealt with the problems of complacent Americans trapped in conformity; *Martin Arrowsmith,* which looked at the lives and problems of physicians; *Elmer Gantry,* which exposed the foibles of some preachers; and *Dodsworth,* which examined the problems of businessmen and manufacturers.

Then the reporter said, "Mr. Lewis, you have been extremely skillful in revealing the nature of the problems of a variety of people. Tell me, Mr. Lewis, do you have any solutions to those problems?"

Lewis leaned back in his rocking chair and ran his long bony fingers through his thinning red hair as he gazed momentarily down the road. Then he replied, "Solutions? No, I don't have any solutions, and furthermore I really don't care."

Upon concluding the interview, the reporter returned to Rome to write his story. In his final statement, he wrote, "Sinclair Lewis will in my judgment never go down in history as a 'great' man. Although greatness does not require that a man have the solutions to all the problems of mankind, greatness does require that a man *care!*"[7]

If Christians are going to become a great people in the face of contemporary problems, they are going to have to learn how to live on the caring level in and through and outside the church.

7. I am indebted to Warren Hultgren, pastor of First Baptist Church, Tulsa, Oklahoma, for this story.

_____ 9 _____

The Transparency
of Self-disclosure

We now go one step deeper to level 7, the sharing level, which is the level of self-disclosure. This is that level where you open yourself to a few confidants you trust and respect and whom you perceive to trust and respect you. You can care for people to whom you may not want to reveal yourself. However, the people to whom you disclose yourself will in all likelihood be people you got to know on the caring level, and if not there, at least on the social-interaction level where you were doing things together on a regular basis.

Caring Enough to Share

To live on the sharing level you have to care enough, for yourself and others, to share with a few people, anywhere from one to a dozen at the most. I have found that for most people on this level the number of confidants ranges from three to five, but this depends on how much time you've had to get to know them.

Because of the intensity likely to be experienced on this level, you shouldn't expect to find many people who qualify to be confidants for you. By sharing your honest feelings, experiences, and expectations, you will be revealing very personal kinds of information. You will become quite vulnerable. Emotionally it's almost like taking off your clothes. Not many people should be expected to qualify by their openness and willingness to listen to, receive, and understand who you are. Some people simply cannot be open to another's sharing of personal information. It frightens them too much. They may feel that they will be expected to reciprocate and they may not be ready for that.

When you confide in some people and they back off, don't take it as personal rejection. They simply are not prepared for it. They are exposing their own fears.

In addition, not many people know how to care about another person. A confidant on the sharing level has to be one who knows how to care, who in attitude is saying, "I care enough about you to listen to your inmost feelings, experiences, and expectations, and to accept whatever you disclose with confidentiality, respect, and concern." Some people are not going to care this much about you. They are bogged down in their own problems and probably overcome with self-pity.

There won't be many who qualify by their ability to receive what you share. They won't know what to do with your disclosures. Some things you share may embarrass them. They are not relationally mature enough to handle the sensitive, personal, and delicate kinds of information that can come out in self-disclosure. Some do not have the ability (actually, the maturity) to keep this kind of information confidential. Confidentiality is essential on the sharing level; otherwise there can be no trust and therefore no openness. You really need to know someone fairly well to know that he or she can keep confidences.

Moreover, the emotional limits of each of us will restrict the number of people with whom we can share. Some people do not have the ego strength to operate on the sharing level. They do just fine on levels 4 and 5, but anything deeper taxes their abilities. On the other hand, I have certain emotional limits. I do not want to share with just anyone or everyone. I can handle only so many confidants myself. Too many confidants will overload my emotional circuits. To trust and confide in everyone or anyone is to water down the meaning and significance of my self-disclosures and the relationships themselves.

How does one find the few who qualify as confidants? I know it sounds trite, but first of all look and listen. There are qualified people around you waiting for you to find them, but they may not know you're looking for them. Who are the people nearest you, emotionally and spiritually, right now? With whom do you associate with on a regular basis and share common interests? Who are the persons toward whom you have most recently reached out in a caring way, and who sought to reciprocate, if only verbally, with deep gratitude? If an emergency or a crisis arose in your life this week, to whom would you most likely turn for help and understanding?

Moreover, in your most personal conversations at coffee breaks, business lunches, or church activities, who gives you the impression that he or she is truly listening to you *and* sharing something of his or her private self? Listen to the way people talk: do they talk only about things and events, or do they talk about feelings? The latter will reveal those most likely to make good confidants.

I am convinced that for the Christian the best confidants will be those with whom you share a lot in common spiritually: your experiences, views, and convictions about God are similar. You will more likely be on the same wavelength. In addition, you will probably have a common understanding of trust, which is crucial on the sharing level.

To find the few who qualify for sharing, you may need to be patient and wait for the right person(s) to come along at the right time. This is something you cannot push. In the meantime, you can test the waters with those who appear to be the most likely prospects. Take the initiative and start sharing some of your thoughts or feelings with another. Those who seem most eager to reciprocate will probably be the best candidates for confidants.

Why care enough to share with some people? What is the need for self-disclosure? For one thing, a great deal of mutual support will be gained from sharing. With the demise of the extended family (parents and grandparents, aunts and uncles, and cousins by the dozens) in this century and the coming of the "secular city," people need a substitute support system that the modern nuclear family (father, mother, and children) usually does not provide. One's confidants on the sharing level become a kind of family support system. On the sharing level you are never alone in facing life's problems and questions.

Confidants become what E. Mansell Pattison calls an "intimate psychosocial kinship system."[1] There are five characteristics of such a system: a high degree of face-to-face interaction; an emotional intensity in which feelings prevail over ideas; the emotions are more positive

1. E. Mansell Pattison, *Pastor and Parish—A Systems Approach*, ed. Howard J. Clinebell, Jr., and Howard W. Stone, Creative Pastoral Care and Counseling series (Philadelphia: Fortress, 1977), p. 18.

than negative; concrete assistance can be counted on if needed; and the relationship is reciprocal.[2]

Therefore, a sort of collective strength is gained on the sharing level. This strength is something everyone needs, especially during times of stress and strain.

I have discovered that when I began to operate on the sharing level, significant spiritual growth—of a quality not experienced on shallower levels—began to take place. This discovery came through my wife's perception of my growth. One cannot easily observe one's own spiritual growth.

What do I mean by spiritual growth? This is very difficult to explain, but I will try. Spiritual growth is a growing awareness of the presence of God leading one's life day by day; a developing faith in the grace and goodness of God even in the face of tragedy, trials, defeats, reversals, and pain; a deepening sensitivity to the mystery of spiritual realities which cannot be subjected to scientific analysis or rational scrutiny (this includes the mystery of the miraculous, the Holy Spirit, the triune nature of God Himself, eternal life, angels, the demonic, the existence of a heaven and a hell, the experience of the new birth, the reality of resurrection, and the reality of the kingdom of God); expanding appreciation for the privilege of prayer and its necessary disciplines; and a broader comprehension of and involvement in a local congregation of fellow believers called a church.

Spiritual growth also includes an increasing excitement over and confidence in the preaching of the gospel of Jesus Christ for evangelization of the non-Christians in the world and the plan of God to reach all nations; a maturing formation of Christ-like character at the core of one's personality which, among other things, causes one to be more open and sensitive to the needs of persons around one and motivates one to reach out to them in closer and more intimate relationships of love and concern; formation of this Christ-like character also results in the development of a biblically informed conscience concerning right and wrong behavior both individually and collectively; a growing awareness of and release to moral and spiritual freedom, which causes one to turn away from legalistic forms of religion to more spontaneous expressions and applications of faith; and a greater and deeper sense of peace with oneself, others, and God, a peace that motivates one to work for peace among nations as well.

2. Ibid., pp. 18–19.

As a summation I list these main points again:

1. Presence of God leading
2. Grace and goodness of God
3. Mystery of spiritual realities
4. Prayer
5. Church
6. Preaching of the gospel
7. Christ-like character and relationships
8. Conscience
9. Freedom
10. Peace
    . . . each in *process*.

You may have a different or better definition of spiritual growth. But I felt the need to spell out in some detail the meaning of that which we rarely define and vaguely assume everyone understands. Try your own hand at writing a definition or explanation. It will be a helpful exercise, especially if you will compare notes in a small group of fellow pilgrims.

Everyone needs to reach the sharing level because everyone has a basic need for a quality of closeness whereby a trusted friend is invited to discover who you are. As you share, you become known, and when known you will be free to be yourself, to be accepted, and loved.

Some reader may be thinking, "Well, if *I* were known, someone would know what a scoundrel I am and would reject me, maybe even fear or hate me, and I couldn't handle that." My response is, no one is a scoundrel in God's eyes. You may act like one from time to time, maybe even most of the time. But you are a person created in the image of God and one for whom Christ died. If you insist on calling yourself a scoundrel, then recognize that God loves scoundrels too.

You should not be loved because of your behavior but rather in spite of it. A Christian confidant will accept you unconditionally. Self-disclosure will be your first step to forgiveness (for whatever your wrong behavior was), cleansing, renewal, and discovery of a new person that you can become in a personal relationship with Jesus Christ.

Paul put it like this: "Therefore, if anyone is in Christ, he is a new creation; the old has gone, the new has come!" (2 Cor. 5:17, NIV). Take a copy of the Bible right now, look up that verse, and read through verse 21. This passage speaks directly to the importance of the sharing level for those who don't feel like sharing out of a dark past.

If you're ever going to be free, you've got to open up, not necessarily revealing all the details of the past (some sins ought to be confessed to God alone), but revealing your need for help in bearing heavy burdens of guilt and frustration (see Gal. 6:2). All of us, regardless of our past, need to move toward achieving depth and closeness with some others. Retaining a certain amount of distance is necessary for normal daily functioning, but remaining distant from everyone is unhealthy.

The Meaning of Trust

To share from deep within, you have to trust another person who accepts and cares about you. What does it mean to trust? How do you do it?

By sharing, I do not mean sharing what you have (money, property, position, things). That kind of sharing takes place on level 6, when specific material needs arise. I am talking here about sharing who you are, not what you have or like to do.

Sharing on level 7 means trusting friends to listen to you: disclosures about your feelings, experiences, frustrations, joys, sorrows, hopes, dreams, defeats, and victories. There is no guarantee that others will listen to you. You have to trust them to do that.

Sharing also means you have to trust these listening friends to understand what you are disclosing, why you are doing so, and how you feel about it. Some people may not be able to understand, because they have no background for understanding your particular experiences, but at least give them the chance to try. Be patient with them. They may need some time to assimilate what you're saying and how you feel.

Sharing is risky, but you have to decide to trust friends to hold your self-disclosures in confidence. When you are revealing material that is especially personal and intimate, simply ask that it be kept confidential. There is no guarantee that it will be, but you have to trust that it will be.

Sharing yourself is making yourself vulnerable to others, but trust is a request for not only understanding and confidentiality, but also support by means of affirmation. A confidant must be trusted not to condemn but to encourage.

Reciprocity may or may not take place in one's efforts at sharing. However, usually trust engenders trust to the point that the friends in whom you confide will want to share in return. I will write more about this later; for now recognize that reciprocity is not the *reason* you share but the *signal* that your trust is being returned and will be honored.

Trusting others with comments about your deepest feelings shows a willingness to be vulnerable. However, remember that vulnerability is a sign of and an invitation to the deeper levels of friendship. If you want deep friendships, you have to run the risks of being hurt. True, your friends can hurt you the most. Who can forget the words of Caesar when he looked at his assassins and cried, "Et tu, Brute!"³ Yet friends are the ones who will love you the most. The element of risk will always be there on the level of sharing.

My experience with the sharing level convinces me that there will be varying trust levels. Factors that determine the level of trust include the persons involved, what is going on in their lives, how long and how well they have known each other, what kinds of experiences they have had in the past with sharing, and their current perceived needs and goals.

Our small prayer-and-share groups in Los Alamos took about two months to develop a deep enough level of trust to reach the sharing level. Even then, the depth of trust varied with each individual. Some people trusted readily; others trusted with great difficulty and took longer. The degree of trust usually depended upon the individual's willingness to risk and to become vulnerable. Once most people reached the sharing level, they were glad they did and chose to stay there with at least one or more persons.

Opening Up and Running Risks

Psychologists have done considerable research and writing on the subject of self-disclosure. The work by Sidney M. Jourard is well worth studying.⁴ This is a subject about which Christians ought to be well informed. The relationship of self-disclosure to the subjects of prayer, counseling, preaching, and evangelism appears obvious, and further study in this regard is loaded with possibilities.

Life for most of us seems to be a poker game, with no one disclosing

3. William Shakespeare, *Julius Caesar*, 3.1.77.
4. See especially Sidney M. Jourard, *The Transparent Self: Self-Disclosure and Well-Being*, 2d ed. (New York: Van Nostrand Reinhold, 1971). Notice his bibliography (pp. 239–45) for additional materials.

his hand to the other players.[5] Instead, he seeks to conceal. If he has
four aces, he hides his hand until the showdown. If he has nothing, he
pretends he has four aces so as to get something for nothing. In our
world which pits person against person, as in a poker game, folks will
keep a poker face. People wear a mask and pretend to be something
they're not. In a relationship where I am *for* you and you are *for* me,
the masks come off.

Surely, we think, people will be open and honest within the family,
but research on the family reveals considerable concealment takes
place even here. At times children do not know their parents, and
parents do not know what the children think or what they're doing.
Husbands and wives are too often found to be strangers one to another
to an unbelievable degree. No wonder most mental illness results from
problems within the family.

How does one get in touch with reality? By knowing the truth. Yet
we are often penalized for disclosing the truth. Impossible goals of
how people ought to live, often heard in legalistic preaching or family
discussions, make most persons so ashamed of themselves that they
feel pressed to seem different, if for no other reason than to protect
their marriages or jobs.

However, when a person does not admit or reveal to himself who,
what, and why he or she is, then that person is out of touch with
reality and in time will become sick. Only the truth can heal. Consequently, health and wholeness can result only as one comes to know
himself or herself, and that is possible only as an outcome of self-
disclosure to another person. Jourard says that this is a basic lesson
learned from psychotherapy (in spite of its limitations): "When a person has been able to disclose himself utterly to another person, he
learns how to increase his contact with his real self, and he may then
be better able to direct his destiny on the basis of this knowledge."[6]

From the perspective of Christian faith, I would add that self-
disclosure in the light of biblical revelation helps one to understand
that his or her true self is incomplete apart from the lordship of Jesus
Christ, who said, "I am the way and the truth [reality] and the life"
(John 14:6, NIV). Coming to know yourself in the context of your need
of Him is to find reality and to discover that your best destiny, according to the Creator's plan, can be guided only by Jesus Christ as

5. This is only an analogy. Gambling in any form is despicable, in my opinion.
6. Jourard, *The Transparent Self*, p. 6.

the Lord of your life. With such assurance, there is absolutely no need for pretense or concealment.

To reveal yourself to a caring and trustworthy Christian confidant (or group) is to allow the true *you* to be known. Self-disclosure means telling someone, "This is what I am: male, age fifty-two, married, white, middle class, educated, professional, teacher, father, husband, son, brother, uncle, Texan, American, religiously conservative, Democrat, writer, preacher, conference leader, jogger." (Refer to chapter 8—my treatment of levels of awareness—on each of the following points.)

Self-disclosure means telling someone, "This is who I am: I see myself as moderately handsome, intelligent, concerned for people, sometimes insecure and lonely, at other times sociable and outgoing; once I had a rather negative self-image but it has become much more positive; I see myself as fairly sensitive to others' wishes, but becoming more concerned about my own objectives in life; my self-confidence is growing year by year; I believe God is directing my life and the lives of my family step by step within a range of freedom; my self-image includes some ambiguity (e.g., both financially secure and insecure); some of my decisions reflect uncertainty (e.g., can I really write a book on this subject that's worth reading?); my self-image at times includes a certain measure of inadequacy; an old rejection syndrome surfaces at times, especially under stress (I know this dates back to a certain event in my childhood which I can now recall, but knowing what caused that syndrome doesn't automatically make it go away). I'm Guy Greenfield, sinner and saint, loved by God, ruled by Christ, but someone with whom God is not yet finished."

Self-disclosure means telling another, "This is where I am: such and such is happening in my family; such and such is happening in my job; such and such is happening in my career; such and such is happening in my friendship circles; such and such is happening to me physically and medically; and here is how I feel about all of this—I feel such and such, and I'd like to know what you think of the way I feel." (I am now being necessarily brief and general. These are things I tell only to confidants, and my readers are not necessarily my confidants. Also, I wish to protect some people.)

Self-disclosure also means telling another, "This is why I am: my religious convictions, beliefs, and opinions as they relate to my life; here is my reason for being, my place in the world, my role in God's plan, my purpose for living, my life goal, all of which I can sum up in my commitment to the will of God revealed in Jesus Christ and obeying Him."

Self-disclosure, moreover, means telling another, "This is what I am saying, what I feel the need to communicate to you at this moment: I feel very lonely and greatly desire your friendship. Consequently, I want to get to know you, so feel perfectly free to tell me what you are, who you are, where you are, why you are, and what you want to say to me. I especially want to hear about your feelings as I hope you will hear about mine."

These levels of self-disclosure are what I call the growing edge of one's personality. The only route to growth I know about is that of self-disclosure. Concealment and pretense result in stagnation. As long as I wear a mask that covers the real me, I do not grow. Change is possible only for those who are open to others in an atmosphere of love and trust.

Self-disclosure does not mean hanging out all your dirty laundry of the past. There is nothing to be gained in that unless a special circumstance calls for it (e.g., you're proposing marriage and you have a child by a previous affair). Telling some things out of a forgiven past might prove detrimental to a new relationship (e.g., you had a homosexual affair once in the army). If God has forgiven such past sins, they should not be retold unless the situation absolutely requires it.

As far as the past is concerned, you can recount those significant peaks and valleys (the victories and defeats) of your life from which you would like to learn lessons for future growth and change. Try this sometime with a friend or in a small sharing group: take a sheet of paper and draw a series of peaks and valleys from childhood to today, identifying each peak (those high points, victories, achievements, significant happy events of your life) and each valley (those low points, defeats, disappointments, reversals, failures, mistakes, significant unhappy events of your life) along with your approximate age when each took place. Then discuss possible lessons you could learn from each event. This kind of self-disclosure of the past has been fruitful for many.

To reveal the present may be the most difficult because it is nearest you. The present is the arena of most of our struggles. There may be guilt over the past and anxiety over the future, but there is nothing like the pain of the present. Here I have in mind, first of all, your present relationships, especially with the significant others in your life, and, second, the most recent events, both positive and negative, you have experienced. The primary purpose of revealing one's present to a trusted confidant is to give you an opportunity to evaluate these relationships and events. What is their real meaning? What are your best alternatives for response?

You will also share your hopes and dreams, goals and objectives. What do you want out of life? Where are you currently headed: in your marriage, in your family, in your vocation, in your faith? If you're not married, are you satisfied to remain single for the foreseeable future? Or are you seriously interested in marrying, but simply haven't met the right person? If you don't have any clear goals and objectives for the various aspects of your life, why not? Would you like to have some targets to shoot at?

What about any fears and anxieties about the future? A fear can be identified; for example, fear of losing your job, cancer, bankruptcy, divorce. Anxiety is a kind of floating fear that cannot be identified specifically. It is a deep uncomfortable feeling about the future, a morbid state of excessive uneasiness. Sharing these feelings with a trusted friend can often help you to get a handle on them: recognizing the sometimes irrational nature of them, identifying the basic fear itself, discovering you have a friend to walk with you into the future.

If your trusted friend is a mature Christian, the experience of sharing one's feelings about the future can often result in finding a deeper confidence in God. I once shared some specific concerns of mine about the future with my pastor at the time, an older and more mature Christian. His response was simply, "Ah yes, I know exactly how you feel. I felt the same way when I was your age. Let me tell you how I dealt with that." His story was exactly what I needed to hear and gave me the confidence to press on.

I have referred to risk in sharing. Risk is a key element in self-disclosure. There is always the possibility of rejection and disappointment. However, I have not often experienced this. After all, by the time you reach this level you pretty well know which of your friends really care and can be trusted. If you are disappointed or rejected, you were probably too hasty in choosing a confidant. The reason why the thought of sharing may scare me is that if I tell you who I really am and you reject me, then I have nothing left to offer you. Rejection comes as a severe blow to my self-image. I would like to avoid that experience of disappointment or embarrassment. But risking is always a vital part of life's major spurts of growth.

Acceptance and appreciation are what I have most often gained from my trusted friends when I opened my heart to them. The risk has brought a greater closeness and companionship. When my wife and I stopped playing games and began to be honest in sharing our deepest feelings, even negative ones, we began to become the close friends we are today.[7]

Risk can be very healthy in developing deeper relationships. You know the old saying, "Nothing ventured, nothing gained." Well, there is a gambler in each of us, not the cheap sort seeking to get something for nothing, but the kind that makes lifetime investments. It was this attitude in the heart of Jesus which Studdert Kennedy captured in his poem, "He Was a Gambler Too . . ."

> And, sitting down, they watched Him there,
> The soldiers did;
> There, while they played with dice,
> He made His Sacrifice,
> And died upon the Cross to rid
> God's world of sin.
> He was a gambler too, my Christ,
> He took His life and threw
> It for a world redeemed.
> And ere His agony was done,
> Before the westering sun went down,
> Crowning that day with its crimson crown,
> He knew that He had won.[8]

The Surprise of Reciprocation

One of the fascinating surprises I found on the sharing level was reciprocation. The people I trusted with my inmost feelings responded by sharing in return. Some professional psychotherapists have learned to use self-disclosure rather than the old Freudian technique of maintaining a disinterested and objective aloofness from the client. Self-disclosure invites the client to confide in the therapist. Disclosure begets disclosure.[9]

I have learned that if I trust you, then you are more likely to trust me. Our prayer-and-share groups at Los Alamos discovered this almost

7. See Eric Berne, *Games People Play* (New York: Ballantine, 1978), and also John W. Drakeford, *Games Husbands and Wives Play* (Nashville: Broadman, 1971).

8. G. A. Studdert Kennedy, *The Unutterable Beauty*, 16th ed. (London: Hodder and Stoughton, 1961), p. 117.

9. Jourard, *The Transparent Self*, pp. 14–16.

immediately as the members reached a level of trust. As individuals began moving away from "here's what happened to me last week" to "here's how I'm feeling this evening," others reciprocated. There seemed to have developed an attitude that said, "If you are willing to trust me with your deepest feelings, than I am willing to trust you with mine." This attitude gradually spread throughout the group.

If you have never done this before, why not give it a try with someone close to you? Experiencing this engendering trust is so much better than merely reading about it.

Generally, I find that people are eager to open up to someone. I would suggest that God made us this way. This natural inclination is best seen among children. A child will tell all to a trusted adult, especially its mother or father. Children seem to have no inhibitions about self-disclosure. Unfortunately, society does a fairly thorough job of building into the human personality all sorts of restrictions, inhibitions, and fears, so that by the time of adulthood we have learned the fine art of concealment and pretense. One way to tap this natural desire for openness is to expose one to openness. Disclosure begets disclosure because people have a primal urge to reveal themselves when they are safe, appreciated, respected, and understood by one who cares. Others need to share as much as you do.

I mentioned in chapter 2 that when I discovered the power of confessional preaching people responded. The reciprocation of the people in my church came as a total surprise to me. My preaching was simply taking on the characteristics of self-disclosure. The point I want to make is that the reciprocation of my people after the services, in small groups in homes, or in private conversations or counseling sessions began a new spurt of spiritual growth for them. They, in effect, were saying, "If our pastor has the same problems, difficulties, and struggles that we do and yet keeps on going, seeking, learning, and discovering, then so can we."As a matter of fact, I even heard them saying to me, "Let's grow together, pastor. Lead the way; we're with you."

Nurturing: A By-product of Going Deeper

When I experienced the dynamics of the caring and sharing levels in my relationships with others, I discovered that I was expressing a more nurturing attitude toward all people and was becoming less judgmental and critical. I began noticing in myself and others that the practice of nurturing was a by-product of going deeper.

As long as people seldom if ever go deeper than level 5, they eventually experience relational deficiency, which in time produces a critical, negative, and judgmental spirit toward others. I call this spirit relational hunger pains. If we really do need each other in close meaningful relationships but do not relate to each other on those deeper levels, then obvious symptoms of this deficiency will appear.

As a young pastor I couldn't understand why there were so many disgruntled church members claiming to be Christians, who could even give glowing testimonies of their conversion, but who expressed more criticism than encouragement, more faultfinding than affirmation, more anger than love. Were these just unconverted church members (converted in the head but not in the heart), "the chaff among the wheat"? Some may have been, but in time I found that most were suffering from relational starvation. They couldn't love very well because they had never been adequately loved by others.

When I criticized them for being critical of me, it just made matters worse. I learned that people who are starving for love aren't helped by more deprivation. There is a futility in being critical of others. Criticism rarely does any good. You might learn some things from it, but there is a better way, Paul's "more excellent way," the way of love. Read 1 Corinthians 13 in a modern translation. People who are critical most of the time are actually crying out, "Why doesn't somebody out there love me?"

The capacity to nurture is developed as a by-product of relational sufficiency, which is achieved on the deeper levels of caring and sharing. The nurturing spirit expresses itself in several ways.

The most obvious way is an expression of encouragement and support. To encourage is to give a person heart (cor). To support means to carry part of the weight, to hold up, to keep from falling or sinking. When you are adequately loved and cared for in close relationships you will have the capacity to give heart to others and help them carry the load and not fall.

Nurturing expresses itself in bringing about togetherness, a sense of family, among people who feel cut off or lonely. The nurturers are the ones who build fellowship in a church. Nurturers rarely have conflicts in marriage. Nurturers attract people, pulling them together.

Nurturing brings about healing of broken relationships. Nurturers are reconcilers, unifiers, and peacemakers. They know how to make

concord out of discord. Nurturers make good nurses and doctors because their attitude encourages the healing of the body. Nurturers
make the best pastors and counselors. They bring strength to people
who are weak or broken. It is the nurturing pastor that a divided
church needs to bring about restoration, reconciliation, and unity of
the fellowship.

Nurturing expresses itself in and through inspiration. A nurturing
person inspires you to be your very best self, to reach for attainable
and worthy goals, to carry plans to completion, and to make dreams
come true. Inspiring people produce inspired people, and both tend to
be very healthy people both mentally and physically.

Amazingly, some contemporary psychologists are showing renewed
interest in "spirit" through some very interesting empirical research.
Jourard even goes so far as to conclude, "I suspect, of course, that
there is a connection between the quality of one's relationships with
significant other people and dispiritation" (his word for loss of spirit,
the will to live, or ultimate discouragement).[10]

The next time you find yourself being critical, negative, or judgmental, stop and examine your relationships. You are probably re-
verting to shallower levels and neglecting the deeper ones. You will
need to go deeper with some other people in your life to recover the
joy of nurturing.

Contexts for Sharing

There is a variety of possible contexts for sharing. Each person
needs to create his or her own best settings. You may already be sharing with someone. If you have at least one close friend you probably
are being transparent with that person now. However, self-disclosure
for you may have been limited to rare instances of crisis in your life
when you felt a desperate need to talk with someone. My suggestion
is that sharing can take on what Jess Lair calls a disposition of mutuality, which is a kind of openness about yourself with whomever you
happen to be in conversation.[11] You will discover that some of these
contacts will eventually develop into deep relationships, but you will

10. Ibid., p. 91. See pp. 80–91 on "Spirit and Wellness."
11. Jess Lair, *I Ain't Well, But I Sure Am Better: Mutual Need Therapy* (New York:
Doubleday, 1975), pp. 94ff.

never know which ones will do so without having a sustained disposition of mutuality. Some contexts will be on an individual basis; others will be in a group.

I think it is natural to share with selected individuals who are open to one's mutuality. Close friends are the logical ones to start with. Youth, especially girls, are usually very good at this with their peers. Teen-age boys are so often caught up in pretending to be macho. I could rarely share with my teen-age male friends because we were so concerned about seeming to be something we weren't. Girls are more open and honest with each other. Adult women tend to carry on with this practice, whereas adult men continue pretending.

I hope you can find at least one close friend you can trust. Everyone needs at least one.

Certainly your marriage provides a natural context for sharing. Your husband or wife ought to be your best friend. If you cannot practice self-disclosure with your mate, then there are probably some deep-rooted barriers in the relationship that need to be confronted, understood, and removed.

You may be wondering if self-disclosure is possible in a parent-child relationship. It is, but this will be the most difficult of all settings. I have found that my parental control demeanor keeps getting in the way. I believe that my overuse of punishment or the threat of it (although I wasn't aware of it at the time) with my children during their early years restrained them as they grew older from reciprocating when I tried to share with them my innermost beliefs and feelings. My children practiced a lot of secrecy right on into their adult years as a result of my heavy parenting during their early years.

I know some parents, however, who are very open with their children and the children with them. They started early in a calm atmosphere of affection and trust. My wife has become better at openness with the children than I. It's still one of my rough edges, although I am trying to change. As soon as the children grow beyond the teen years, parents are wise to gradually shift from being parents to being friends. I wish that I had a relational recipe for doing that. Maybe knowing it needs to be done is a good start, a goal toward which to move.

The most exciting experience Carole and I have had with sharing has been in the small-group setting in our Los Alamos congregation. What I consider the ideal structure is a group ranging from six to

twelve persons. Our Los Alamos groups had six couples. We realized
that average participation would be eight to ten persons per meeting.
No group will average 100 percent attendance. We reasoned that if
Jesus thought that a maximum size for an intensive group should be
twelve, then there must be good reason. Most would agree that beyond
twelve a group becomes unwieldly and loses the dynamic of a small
group.

A small sharing group needs some structure and a convener if not
a leader. I found it best for leadership to float among the group members. The group needs to state and agree upon its purpose, goals,
methods, and termination, and have some time for evaluation and
discussion of future possibilities. Apart from some minimal structure
and direction, informality and a relaxed atmosphere are very important. It is wise for a new sharing group to study some of the helpful
books on small-group experiences. See the list of suggested readings
at the end of this chapter.

Some small groups may wish to operate on a short-term basis for
an initial experiment. Our first groups met for only four months, once
a week, after which they evaluated their experiences and decided their
future. In time, some groups may wish to establish a long-term relationship. The Los Alamos groups have continued for several years with
various breaks, vacations, and reorganization.

Our groups always met in the relaxed atmosphere of a group member's home rather than at the church building. Meetings were rotated
among the members' homes. Place is important. Also, no children
should be present; arrange for them to be elsewhere.

I have said that the church usually is not programed for deepening
relationships. This is unfortunate. The first churches were necessarily
small and met in homes. This provided for the possibilities of closeness. But today so many churches are programed for bigness. Consequently, if today's church is going to encourage intimacy, closeness,
deeper relationships, and meaningful friendships, then the key to such
provision will be the leadership of the pastor, his staff, and official
board. If they are not aware of the need and the possibilities, probably
nothing will happen.

The church's leadership will need the necessary skills to develop
closeness in the congregation. But these skills can be learned just as
any skills can be learned. A great deal has been written on the subject

of small groups. In addition, it would be good to visit a church where a small-group sharing ministry is functioning effectively.[12]

The church should create opportunities for developing close relationships. Lay people are eagerly waiting for church leaders to design worship services that emphasize relationships rather than passive listening. Bible-study classes need to be kept small, and teaching therein should be more relational, participatory, and less lecture-oriented. Prayer-and-share groups can be started if people are given proper leadership. Ministry groups established for meeting targeted needs of people are another possibility. The possibilities are unlimited. The problem is usually leadership. What are you doing about your church? Don't just complain—do something. Studying this book in a small group for twelve weeks would be a good place to start.

A Theology for Sharing

Christians have a great heritage for developing relationships on the sharing level. Mentioning a few examples will suffice.

From the beginning, God shares His creative powers with mankind. Four commands of God in creation reveal His sharing: nature, wherein God shares His bounty of all good things; marriage, in which God shares His love and the creation of life in and through sexuality; the state, in which God shares His authority and power; and the church, in which God shares Himself in the gospel of His Son.

As we look more specifically at some of the great biblical truths, we may further observe the divine sharing. In the incarnation, God shared with us His Son. "The Word became flesh and lived for a while among us. We have seen his glory, the glory of the only Son, who came from the Father, full of grace and truth" (John 1:14, NIV). The concept of closeness is certainly reflected in the phrase *the Word became flesh.*

The biblical concept of redemption conveys the idea of buying back. It was a common practice in biblical times for a master to purchase a slave on the auction block for the purpose of setting him free. The biblical writers thought of this illustration when interpreting the sal-

12. See Robert C. Girard, *Brethren, Hang Loose, Or What's Happening to My Church?* (Grand Rapids: Zondervan, 1972); and Lawrence O. Richards, *A New Face for the Church* (Grand Rapids: Zondervan, 1981) and *Three Churches in Renewal* (Grand Rapids: Zondervan, 1975).

vation God brought to man in Jesus Christ. Therein God shares His love and grace in our new freedom *from* sin and *to* eternal life.

God has not remained hidden from us. He has revealed Himself in the person of His Son. "No one has ever seen God, but God the only Son, who is at the Father's side, has made him known" (John 1:18, NIV). In revelation God shares Himself and His truth.

The doctrine of last things, or eschatology, teaches that this life is not the end of God's story. History is going somewhere: the goal is the ultimate reign of God over the whole universe. In the end, God will share His eternal home with His people. The best is yet to be.

Finally, I want to call to your attention some biblical examples of sharing. Several come to mind. The relationship of Jonathan and David was especially close, so much so that one verse says, "Jonathan became one in spirit with David, and he loved him as himself" (1 Sam. 18:1, NIV). The account in chapters 18–20 of 1 Samuel reveals a deep relationship between these two friends; such depth of relationship is rarely described in the Old Testament stories of Israel.

I am also reminded of the apostle John's unusually close relationship with Jesus. He referred to himself as "the disciple whom Jesus loved" (John 13:23; 19:26; 20:2; 21:7, 20, NIV). These five references certainly do not mean that Jesus did not love the other disciples; rather, John was suggesting a very special and close relationship which I suspect approximated the sharing level if not the intimacy level.

Finally, there is Paul, who so often shared his very soul with his churches, as we see in his letters. One of the most revealing passages is 2 Corinthians 12:1–10 where, as many scholars believe, Paul was sharing an autobiographical insight into a most unusual spiritual experience. And who could overlook the very deep relationship Paul had with Timothy? Their sharing must have been far beyond the usual relationship among the early Christians.

Suggested Readings

Bangham, William. *The Journey into Small Groups.* Memphis, TN: Brotherhood Commission, SBC, 1974.

Clemmons, William, and Harvey Hester. *Growth Through Groups.* Nashville: Broadman, 1974.

Clinebell, Howard J., Jr. *The People Dynamic: Changing Self and Society Through Growth Groups.* New York: Harper and Row, 1972.

Leslie, Robert C. *Sharing Groups in the Church: An Invitation to Involvement.* Nashville: Abingdon, 1979.

Neighbor, Ralph. *The Journey into Discipleship.* Memphis, TN: Brotherhood Commission, SBC, 1974.

Oden, Thomas C. *The Intensive Group Experience: The New Pietism.* Philadelphia: Westminster, 1972.

Southard, Samuel. *Your Guide to Group Experience.* Nashville: Abingdon, 1974.

10

The Deepest Level of All

A few months ago I was discussing levels of interpersonal relationships with members of an adult class in a Dallas church. Having been invited to speak about relationships, I decided to elicit their reactions to the ideas in this book. At that time I had developed the concept of only seven levels. When I finished explaining the seventh level and asked for their response, one young woman declared, "There has to be an eighth level. Seven isn't quite deep enough. I'm not sure what to call it, but there is a deeper level, and some get there with only one or two people. Some unusual people may get there with a few more."

The entire group agreed and after discussing it a while I asked, "Are we talking about intimacy?" Someone responded, "That's it!" The eighth level is the intimacy level, the deepest level of all.

For some time I had felt uneasy about finishing my analysis of relationships with the sharing level. I suspected that and wondered if there could be an eighth level. I knew that my relationship with Carole was more than open, honest, and deep sharing. My Dallas friends helped me to identify the intimacy level with a name and a description.

This is not an easy chapter to write. I am describing a level that is very difficult to explain. In translating one's experience to language, some of it inevitably gets lost in translation. To understand intimacy to any degree, you must experience it for yourself. But as I write, I hope I can at least point the way.

The Mathematics of the Deepest Level

You are probably familiar with the verses in Genesis which refer to the union of man and woman in marriage: "For this reason a man will leave his father and mother and be united to his wife, and they will become one flesh. The man and his wife were both naked, and they felt no shame" (Gen. 2:24–25, NIV). Now I realize that the one-flesh relationship in marriage is a unique and special thing, and that the term carries a clear sexual connotation. However, the oneness of the one-flesh relationship is certainly suggestive of the closeness I have found on the intimacy level where, in a psychological and emotional sense, two become, as it were, one. On the intimacy level, one plus one equals one.

By referring to the statement in Genesis that the two shall become one, I am not suggesting that marriage automatically brings one to the intimacy level. Neither am I suggesting that the physical intimacy of sexual relations provides one with access to intimacy. Obviously, there are a lot of marriages and a lot of sex where there is no intimacy in this deeper sense to which I am referring.

Of course, the most logical person with whom you can reach the intimacy level is your spouse. The initial oneness of marriage would naturally provide some fertile soil for the growth of intimacy. This was where I discovered the eighth level, but it took several years after we married to reach it.

However, I also believe that one can achieve the oneness of the intimacy level with persons other than one's spouse; in these relationships sex has absolutely nothing to do with closeness. Why not an unusually close friend, male or female? Why not even God?

There is no clear exegetical way to prove this, but I suspect that the relationships of Jonathan and David, Jesus and John, and Paul and Timothy (referred to in chapter 9 as biblical examples of sharing) somehow approximated the intimacy level.

How does one describe the oneness of intimacy? The person or persons to whom we relate on the eighth level we will also relate to on the other levels from time to time, certainly on the caring and sharing levels. Experience on the sharing level with a person will be necessary preparation for moving on to the intimacy level with that person. Intimacy clearly involves deep sharing of one's innermost experiences and feelings.

Intimacy calls for transparency: total honesty couched in love. Intimacy involves the deepest possible trust, believing that the other person has your best interests at heart and would never think of violating that trust. Intimacy expresses itself in the deepest altruistic concern for the other. Empathy prevails throughout the relationship. Touching each other on this level is as natural as speaking. As a matter of fact, touching, whether a handclasp or a bear hug, is a form of speaking on the intimacy level. On this level you can touch or look into each other's eyes and clearly communicate, never having spoken a word. Incidentally, I believe that certain ways of looking at each other are forms of both touching and communicating. A wink of the eye can be either an invitation to or an expression of intimacy.

Intimacy can be expressed by the tone of one's voice. To me the noun *softness* describes the intimate communication, whether it be a quiet comment, a humorous expression, a word of sorrow, or joyful laughter as one relates to another on this level. Such conversation conveys an almost private tone. It is a quality of communication only for someone very special.

The oneness of intimacy is much more than intellectual agreement or relational unity. Intimacy is possible with someone with whom you may disagree on certain opinions, beliefs, or convictions. Two people can continue to be unique and separate individuals yet one in spirit. Such oneness involves total acceptance with no judgmental reservations or subtle plans to change the other.

The Ultimate Knowledge of Another

When I refer to the intimacy level of relating, I must admit that I'm at a slight loss for words to write what I mean. We have so few words in our language to describe intimacy: closeness, love, affection, understanding, empathy, sexual relations, courtship, comforting, compassion. Yet each of these words has certain limitations. Each word could mean different things to different people. Each word could suggest a matter of degree and has to be qualified by some adjective which is also limited: for example, deep love.

When I try to describe intimacy I could say that I'm referring to the experience of *really* knowing a person and *really* being known by that person. But what do I mean by *really*? Fully? Totally? Is such knowledge possible? Is anything or anyone ever fully and completely known by imperfect minds? By using the word *really*, I suppose I'm grasping for a superlative that expresses the deepest possible relationship. Yet have I actually described it?

The ultimate knowledge of another person is in all likelihood a relative matter, depending upon what there is to know and how much is revealed. Some folks are very plain and simple while others are quite complex. Whatever is to be known, however, has to be revealed either directly or indirectly. My wife knows things about me that I do not know about myself. She can see things in me that I do not see. Such traits are revealed, although indirectly, in the way I act or talk: the expression on my face, my stance, tone of voice, or general demeanor.

Ideally, the ultimate knowledge of another can be revealed to another out of our deepest thoughts, feelings, experiences, hopes and dreams, fears and frustrations. This is why sharing is a basic prerequisite for intimacy.

The biblical verb *to know*, interestingly, is used occasionally to describe ultimate sexual knowledge of another.[1] Some scholars suggest that such usage is a euphemism, the substitution of a mild or indirect term for a direct one. Even the term *intimacy* is used by some people today as a substitute for the phrase *sexual intercourse*. However, I suspect that the biblical verb *to know* is more than a euphemism for sexual relations. When a man "knows" a woman sexually he is gaining a knowledge of her that is deeply intimate, personal, and special, and which can be gained in no other way. A line in a recent movie says, "After you've had sex, a relationship is never the same." That is very true. This kind of knowledge is much more than physical.

The biblical word *to know* or its cognates is used in Scripture to refer to more than a physical kind of knowledge. Naturally, most of the time the word is used regarding knowing facts or specific information. But several references indicate that it implies a deeper personal, psychological, or emotional insight into the heart of another. A study of a complete concordance will reveal several such usages (e.g., Ps. 139:1–6, 23; Isa. 19:21; Jer. 31:34; John 1:31, 33; 2:25; 10:14; 1 Cor. 2:11, 16; 8:3; Gal. 4:8–9). This kind of personal knowing of another is to know something of what the other is thinking, feeling, desiring, planning, hoping, dreaming, anticipating, and longing for without necessarily being told in so many words. It is the closeness of human spirit with human spirit and is not necessarily limited by geographical distance or difference in age.

1. The references are Genesis 4:1, 17, 25; 19:8; 24:16; 38:26; Numbers 31:17, 18, 35; Judges 11:39; 19:25; 21:11, 12; 1 Samuel 1:19; 1 Kings 1:4; Matthew 1:25. The same word can refer to the sin of sodomy: Genesis 19:5; Judges 19:22.

The Dimensions of Intimacy

Howard and Charlotte Clinebell have written an important and helpful book about intimacy in marriage.[2] They have identified several dimensions of intimacy, which they compare to the several strings of a musical instrument. Marital music is made by playing on a variety of combinations of these strings. A couple's particular harmony and melody of intimacy are what *they* find most satisfying in the various periods of their marriage. There will be times when there will be disharmony or even silence. The dimensions are dynamic, not static.

Sexual intimacy. In marriage, sexual intimacy is the hub around which all forms of intimacy gather. Marriage provides the best setting for developing the optimum blend of the sensual-emotional pleasures of sex. Sexual intimacy, as God planned it—and it was His idea—is so much more than the union of sexual organs, or the physical arousal of a husband and wife, or the achievement of orgasm. It is the total fulfillment of two persons, as expressed by the term *becoming one flesh.*

Emotional intimacy. When two people become tuned into each other's emotional wavelengths by sharing their inner worlds of meaning and feeling, they achieve emotional intimacy. Such couples often sense what each other is feeling even before any words are spoken. The emotional dimension could even be called the foundation of all the other forms of intimacy. Emotional intimacy might be described not as the touching of the hands but the touching of the hearts of each other.

Intellectual intimacy. When two close friends share their world of ideas with mutual benefit, they are achieving intellectual intimacy. This is the sharing of mind-stretching experiences: reading stimulating books, studying issues of common interest and concern, discussing a stirring lecture or a heavy drama or a probing movie. Such intimacy is based on mutual respect for the intellectual capacities of each. Having similar educational backgrounds is important for achieving this dimension of intimacy.

Aesthetic intimacy. A deep sharing of various experiences of beauty can lead to the dimension of aesthetic intimacy, whether it be the sharing of the moving strains of a marvelous symphony, the sight of the sun sparkling on the waves crashing upon a sandy beach, walking

2. Howard J. Clinebell, Jr., and Charlotte H. Clinebell, *The Intimate Marriage* (New York: Harper and Row, 1970), pp. 28ff.

through a forest of giant sequoia, observing the fury of a mountain storm, or basking in the glowing orange and red colors of a sunset. Beauty is a matter of taste, so each couple must find what suits their own tastes.

Creative intimacy. Sharing in acts of creating something worthwhile together can bring creative intimacy. Conceiving and parenting children, landscaping the yard, planting a garden, composing a piece of music, or one supporting the other in some masterful achievement are illustrations of creative intimacy. Such intimacy provides the dynamic for helping each other grow: becoming co-creators and re-creators of each other, "engaged in the mutuality of feeding the heart hungers of each other so that each can realize his potentialities as a person."

Recreational intimacy. To relate together in experiences of fun and play on a deep level is to accomplish recreational intimacy. For newlyweds this may involve a great deal of sexual intimacy. In time, recreation broadens to include a wide variety of enjoyable interests and activities. Such intimacy is essential to the growth of a meaningful relationship, not to mention the mental health of the persons involved. To use a term from transactional analysis, recreational intimacy allows one's child to run free and rejuvenate the self through stress-relieving play.

Work intimacy. The closeness of sharing common tasks can bring about work intimacy. Building a house or a business, raising a family, earning a living, and participating in community projects provide opportunities for achieving this dimension of intimacy. Working to assist a son or daughter graduate from college and launch a career is a rewarding experience of work intimacy.

Crisis intimacy. Closeness in coping with problems and pain can bring strength not to be found anywhere else. Standing together against tragedy is often an experience of intimate suffering. Crisis intimacy can also take place in a marriage where conflict seems to erupt more often than usual as the couple painfully adjusts to serious personality differences. Conflict can draw a couple closer together. Resolved conflict can cement marriage ties, as well as those in other types of relationships.

Commitment intimacy. It is also possible for two people to derive a unique form of mutuality from common self-investment. When two close friends share a dedication to some cluster of values or a cause that is bigger than either of them, and they regard this commitment as worth working for, they will experience commitment intimacy.

"Being captured by a common cause that turns on enthusiasm and conviction provides a powerful bond in a marriage" or a friendship.

Spiritual intimacy. The we-ness in sharing ultimate concerns may be called spiritual intimacy. Ultimate concerns are the meaning of life, one's relationship to the universe and to God, as well as a basic purpose in life. The sense of a transcendent relatedness may provide a firm foundation or supportive ground for transient human relatedness. Involvement in one's church and in the larger Christian endeavor (missions, evangelism, Christian ministry, or social action) can stimulate and nurture the development of spiritual intimacy when that involvement is shared with another or others.

Communication intimacy. The source of all types of true intimacy is described as communication intimacy. This dimension involves understanding not only each other's words but also feelings, intentions, and motives. Such intimacy may reach a level where nonverbal communication is as common as verbal between the two. Depth in closeness brings greater understanding.

The Clinebells conclude their discussion of the dimensions of intimacy by pointing out that each dimension has the potential for drawing married partners together. These dimensions allow opportunities for the lives of two people to touch significantly in a growing number of areas of human experience. Intimacy produces we-ness, which is a form of shared identity and mutual commitment to one another. This complementary interaction brings about a gradual narrowing of the emotional distance between two people until there is "a genuine interlocking of personalities," a kind of psychological union.[3]

The Creation of Intimacy

Does intimacy just happen? I believe that intimacy is created, brought about by desire and choice. I have already said that certain commonalities, considerable caring, and intensive sharing are prerequisites for intimacy. I further believe that a strong, positive, and wholesome self-image is also a prerequisite for each of two people who achieve intimacy. A person whose self-image is weak, negative, and poor will generally avoid or be unable to create intimacy, because he will fear closeness and possible rejection.

3. Ibid., p. 32. See also the Clinebells' Marital Intimacy Checkup and Action Plan, pp. 37–39.

Other possible prerequisites to intimacy are a feeling of inner security or self-confidence and a clear conscience. Insecure people who lack confidence in themselves and God (the source of inner security) and who are always struggling with unresolved guilt find it difficult if not impossible to create intimacy.

Only people with strong egos try to establish intimate relationships. A strong, positive self-image has a high tolerance for the pain of rejection. Ego strength is needed to be able to handle the intensity of intimacy. People with weak egos prefer to hide in the shallower levels of relating: avoidance, greeting, or separate and common interests.

How do the people with strong and positive self-images create intimacy with a few close friends? For one thing, they limit themselves to a very *few*: one to three on an average, maybe five for the unusually strong and experienced. The very concept suggests that only a few are involved. There is a certain restrictiveness involved in the process itself.

I can refer to only my own experience with intimate relationships, primarily with my wife. We have learned to create intimacy by accentuating our common interests, by specific and regular instances of caring, by times of intensive sharing (mostly of our deepest feelings), and by special times of giving ourselves to each other. We are still in the process of learning to enjoy each other and accept pleasure into our lives. This latter point has been especially difficult for me because, for some unknown reason, I have long felt that I do not deserve pleasure in my life, especially if anyone knows it.

Carole and I have also concentrated on gift-giving, which can be one tangible means of expressing intimacy if the gift is particularly personal. She is much better at this than I. I have never felt very qualified to select a personal gift for her, especially clothes, because I rarely feel any certainty about sizes, preferences, and matching of colors. Gift-giving is normally done on special occasions (birthdays, anniversaries, Christmas) and this is important, but the very best kind of gift-giving is on those "no-particular-reason" days when the gift comes as a total surprise simply as an expression of love.

The first time I sent Carole flowers "for no special reason," the other people in her office, after discovering it wasn't her birthday or our wedding anniversary, were so caught off guard that they kidded her about the fight we must have had that morning or my feeling guilty over something. The truth was that it was neither a peace offering nor a guilt offering. Her friends at the office simply could not believe that

it was merely a surprise love offering. Some of the women went home
and chided their husbands for never doing anything like that. Some
of those husbands never forgave me for the "trouble" I caused them
at home!

Another avenue to intimacy seems to me to be touching and being
touched. Science has taught us that the skin is as much an organ of
the body as is the heart.[4] As a matter of fact, it is a crucial organ:
third-degree burns over too much of the body's surface can kill a person, because the skin's breathing function is destroyed. The skin is
very much alive with nerve endings that are extremely sensitive to
heat and cold, pins and needles, hands and fingers.

Touching is a form of communication, whether a caress, a hug, or
holding hands. This is a big part of being human. Who can teach us
the importance of human touching? Children. We can learn a lot about
the intimacy of touching from watching a child relate to a parent or
to another child. Children love to touch and be touched. This is seen
in their loving to be picked up and hugged or carried. However, sad
as it is to say it, in time cultural conditioning almost destroys this
natural urge to be touched, although I believe the desire remains.

The fear of touching has especially permeated most of British and
American culture. This is particularly true when it comes to touching
members of the opposite sex. My wife was taught quite early not to
touch boys and to *never* let a boy touch her, especially if they were
alone. Even several years into adulthood she retained this deeply in-
grained inhibition. In the early years of our marriage it almost ruined
our sex life. Emotional inhibitions gained from authority figures have
an unusually long life and are stubbornly resistant to change.

Fear, distance, and alienation have all but destroyed the gift of
touching. I laughed out loud when I first read about Leo Buscaglia's
experience on elevators:

> If you want to see how alienated we've become, watch when a door
> of an elevator opens. Everyone's standing like zombies, facing straight
> forward, hands to the sides. "Don't you dare reach this way because you
> may touch someone." Heaven forbid! So we all stand at attention and
> the door opens and then one gets out and another goes in and turns
> around immediately and faces forward. Who told you you had to face
> forward? You know, I love to walk in an elevator and turn around with

4. A fascinating study on this subject is Ashley Montagu's *Touching: The Human
Significance of the Skin* (New York: Columbia University, 1971).

my back to the door! And I look at everybody and I say, "Hi! Wouldn't it be marvelous if the elevator got stuck and we could all get to know each other?" And then an incredible thing happens. The door opens on the next floor and everybody gets off! "There's a crazy man in the elevator. He wants to know us!"[5]

What about adults touching members of the opposite sex? Well, of course, it all depends upon several elements in the situation. You don't just rush up and hug a person you've never met before. The message will be too garbled. He or she, not knowing you, will have no basis for understanding what you are saying. Some acquaintance and degree of friendship are necessary to clarify your intentions and message. A warm, friendly, and firm (but not bone-crushing!) handclasp is almost always appropriate. If you have reached at least the sixth level (caring) of relating with someone, a gentle hug (or an arm-around-the-shoulder kind of hug) is certainly appropriate if you wish to affirm your friendship upon greeting. For Christians who know one another, what would be the problem here? If the early Christians could greet one another with a holy kiss, why can we not greet one another with a "holy hug" today?

In Los Alamos our church grew into a hugging church. Not *every* person, but a good many, had no inhibitions about touching each other. When people see their pastor touch or hug women of all ages in public, it helps to break down the barriers. Several of the men would often hug my wife or put an arm around her shoulder upon entering the building or following a worship service. I seriously doubt if an immoral sexual thought ever passed through our minds. We truly cared for each other and felt comfortable in sharing our spiritual affection as members of the body of Christ.

I strongly suspect that much of the stress on the cultural prohibitions of "don't touch, don't handle, don't look" actually stimulates immoral thoughts and brings about many of the very things those rules were created to prevent. This principle would apply to some church summer camps that still prohibit mixed swimming. It is as though some people have never read Paul's words on this subject:

Why ... do you submit to its rules: "Do not handle! Do not taste! Do not touch!"? These are all destined to perish with use, because they are

5. Leo Buscaglia, *Living, Loving, and Learning,* ed. Steven Short (New York: Fawcett Columbine, 1982), p. 30.

based on human commands and teachings. Such regulations indeed have
an appearance of wisdom, with their self-imposed worship, their false
humility and their harsh treatment of the body, but they lack any value
in restraining sensual indulgence. [Col. 2:20b–23, NIV]

One can be very lustful and never touch another person. Lust is a
strong desire for anything that is outside of the will of God: money
that one steals, sex outside of marriage, or food beyond one's normal
bodily needs.

Touching can be practiced on several different levels of relating, but
it is most appropriate on the intimacy level to express a sincere and
deeply meaningful affection for one another. My experience on this
level, as I stated earlier, has largely although not totally been limited
to my wife in recent years, and I am still trying to learn how to express
myself on this level. But it is possible to achieve intimacy with other
adults in one's life, even those of the same sex. If you have a problem
with this, I suggest you read about and consider the relationship of
David and Jonathan (1 Sam. 20:35–42, especially v. 41).[6]

Intimacy can also be expressed by the use of the eyes. There are
several ways to look at another person: with anger, lust, pity, compassion, disappointment, and affection. An affectionate look expresses
intimacy. This nonverbal communication says, "I am very glad to see
you, to know you are here. Your very presence brings joy to my heart,
a smile to my face, a spring to my step, and music to my thoughts. I
highly value you. Your presence is a complement to my personality.
You bring out the best in me, and I think I bring out the best in you.
We are good for each other. Life is much richer because of our relationship, which among many things deepens my hope in the future."

Looking is very important in communicating closeness and love.
Remember Emily in *Our Town*? "Nobody looks at anybody. Nobody
cares anymore, do they?"

Another avenue to intimacy is regularly praying together with close
friends. When I was a sophomore in college I developed a close friendship with another student whom I met at church and the Baptist
Student Center. It wasn't long before Roger and I agreed to become
prayer partners. The idea had been suggested by our Baptist Student

6. Some authors try to make a case for the idea that David and Jonathan were
homosexuals. This is nothing but foolish speculation based upon distorted exegesis
and cultural analysis that reasons from the general to the specific. See, for example,
Tom Horner, *Jonathan Loved David: Homosexuality in Biblical Times* (Philadelphia:
Westminster, 1978), pp. 26–39.

Union director one evening at vespers. Roger and I met in a small study room at the Student Center at noon one day a week to pray for a variety of needs in our lives, in the lives of our friends, and in the church. This experience, lasting several months, brought us together in a oneness that produced some needed significant changes in my life, and which I have never forgotten.

A small group of men met every Tuesday morning in our church in Los Alamos to pray together for about twenty minutes before going on to work. Praying together for several years has created an extremely deep closeness among these men. The many prayer-and-share groups in the congregation there experienced a similar spiritual intimacy. For Christians the promised presence of our common Lord explains the dynamic behind such intimacy: "For where two or three come together in my name, there am I with them" (Matt. 18:20, NIV).

For Marriage Only?

Some readers may be wondering if intimate relationships ought not be limited to marriage. I have already suggested that intimacy is possible with friends other than one's spouse and of both sexes. Yet some may fear that this is unwise, because it possibly leads to either extramarital or homosexual affairs.

First of all, I want to declare unequivocally that I believe that any extramarital affair is morally wrong and relationally detrimental to everyone involved either directly or indirectly. Adultery is adultery regardless of whatever else one calls it and is strictly forbidden by the Word of God (Exod. 20:14; Matt. 5:27–28).

Second, I wish to make it clear that I believe that homosexuality is not a third-gender condition with which one is born but is a learned sinful behavior and lifestyle, although with several complex relational variables at work. One can change by way of repentance, conversion, counseling by competent professionals, and the help of a heterosexual support group of caring Christians. God's Word condemns homosexual behavior and calls for repentance and commitment to Christ (Rom. 1:18–32, especially vv. 26–27; 1 Cor. 6:9–11; 1 Tim. 1:8–11). This clearly implies that one can change a homosexual orientation to a heterosexual one.[7]

7. For further reading that supports my position on this subject, see David Field, *The Homosexual Way—A Christian Option?* (Downers Grove, IL: Inter-Varsity, 1979); John W. Drakeford, *A Christian View of Homosexuality* (Nashville: Broadman, 1977); and Richard F. Lovelace, *Homosexuality and the Church* (Old Tappan, NJ: Revell, 1978).

I have said all that to say this: it is possible to sin at any level of relating. Consequently, the intimacy level is no more a risk outside of marriage than the sharing or social-interaction levels. Personal moral integrity and mutual respect should be in every Christian's lifestyle as guardians against wrong behavior. Temptations to do wrong may be found on any level of relating. Actually, a thesis of this book is that the deeper one goes in interpersonal relationships, the greater dynamic one will find to live the Christian life. This assumes all the other elements are present: that is, a new birth, a maturing discipleship, and the power of the Holy Spirit in one's life.

I think it helps to recognize that adults can experience different types of intimacy. When one relates to one's spouse, there will obviously be the more tender expressions, verbal and nonverbal symbols of a special nature unknown to others, unique times and places, as well as sexual intimacy. When one relates to members of the same sex or members of the opposite sex other than one's spouse, there will be those special moments of close friendship involving deep communication and understanding but with no sexual overtones or behavior involved—much as parents and their adult children or brothers and sisters would relate to each other. Paul spoke in this way when he advised Timothy to treat an older man as a father and to "treat younger men as brothers, older women as mothers, and younger women as sisters, with absolute purity" (1 Tim. 5:1–2, NIV). The phrase *absolute purity* indicates the moral integrity and mutual respect needed.

One bit of advice might be helpful for those who are inexperienced in dealing with intimacy. The married person who reaches this level with a person of the opposite sex ought to relate to that person openly and honestly along with his or her own spouse and the spouse of the other person if at all possible. Couples are often uniquely equipped to relate to each other on this level. For some persons sexual temptation may be a factor to carefully guard against: never meet privately or without one's mate's knowledge and always share this level *as couples*. If sexual temptation enters the picture, then retreat and find out why it has and what is going on emotionally in your own marriage. A happily married Christian whose sexual needs are being met by his or her spouse will very rarely be tempted sexually. However, if sexual temptations persist, a clinically trained pastor or a professional marriage counselor should be consulted to determine the reasons, for these are often subconscious.

The Need for Privacy

People who relate on the intimacy level should not overlook every person's need for some privacy. There are times when every one of us needs to be alone in order to evaluate recent decisions, attitudes, and actions. You are responsible for you. No one else is. Moreover, each one of us needs those special times to get off by himself and walk in the woods, dangle his feet in a cold stream or lake, sit under a tree in the back yard and watch the birds, or do whatever recharges the batteries.

Lois Wyse beautifully describes the need to balance intimacy with autonomy, especially in one's marriage:

> There is within each of us
> A private place
> For thinking private thoughts
> And dreaming private dreams.
>
> But in the shared experience of marriage,
> Some people cannot stand the private partner.
>
> How fortunate for me
> That you have let me grow,
> Think my private thoughts,
> Dream my private dreams.
>
> And bring a private me
> To the shared experience of marriage.[8]

I need time to think and to ask myself from time to time some basic questions. What am I doing? Where am I going? Should I be making some changes in my life? How can I develop my talents and skills? Is my life making a wholesome difference to those around me? If not, why not? What is God trying to say to me at this time in my life? Is His will being worked out for and in my life? If not, how can I make a midcourse correction? These are questions to be asked and answered in my solitude. Others may help, but only after I've done my own homework. People involved in an intimate relationship will respect the need for solitude.

Moreover, there is a need to balance privacy and intimacy. They ought to go together. My wife and I have worked out this balance

8. Lois Wyse, *Love Poems for the Very Married* (Cleveland: World Publishing, 1967), p. 51. Used by permission.

fairly well in our own relationship. I respect her private times, and she respects mine, but then we come together again in intimacy. Paul once referred to this need, although he was specifically dealing with the issue of sexual intimacy and prayer. Nevertheless, the principle is the same. "Do not deprive each other [sexually] except by mutual consent and for a time, so that you may devote yourselves to prayer. Then come together again so that Satan will not tempt you because of your lack of self-control" (1 Cor. 7:5, NIV).

Being Understood and Understanding Another

The intimacy level provides tremendous resources for living. Knowing that I am understood by at least one other person who truly cares about me greatly shores up my ability to face anything life brings. It's also a good feeling, a rewarding sense of purpose, to know that my deep understanding of another does the same in return.

There is comfort in being understood by an intimate friend. You know that in your situation, whatever that may be at the time of sharing, you are not alone. Being understood brings company. Not long ago, I had had a very bad day at work. Nothing seemed to go right. Every time I turned around I was making a mistake, causing a problem, or facing some kind of criticism. I had *had* it. I packed my briefcase and went home early just to get away from it all. When Carole came home from work she perceived immediately that something was wrong. She could tell I was depressed, angry, and lonely. She curled up beside me on the couch, put her arm around me, and said, "Tell me all about it." I told her about the entire day. She understood. I felt comfort because I was no longer alone. She understood and shared my frustration.

Moreover, there is strength in being understood by an intimate friend. In our first prayer-and-share group in Los Alamos, Carole and I approached the intimacy level with three couples. At that particular time we were having some serious problems with one of our children. We told these dear friends the whole story. We were almost devastated and needed help. Each couple responded almost identically, "We understand. We've had similar problems with one of our children. Let us share the burden with you." They understood, cared, and reached out to hold us up. We began to feel their strength.

There is also joy in being understood. I am learning that on the intimacy level there is a joy not found on any of the other levels. There is satisfaction in caring (level 6), there is relief in sharing (level 7), but there is joy in being deeply understood by an intimate friend (level 8). It is the joy of two people sharing their deepest needs and each knowing the other both cares and understands. Aloneness is replaced by togetherness.

The most moving illustration of two people who reached the intimacy level is the story of Robert and Elizabeth Barrett Browning. The love of these two for each other is expressed throughout their poetry. What Elizabeth thought of Robert may be found in her *Sonnets from the Portuguese*, addressed to him before their marriage. Who can forget these immortal lines?

> How do I love thee? Let me count the ways.
> I love thee to the depth and breadth and height
> My soul can reach, when feeling out of sight
> For the ends of Being and ideal Grace.
> I love thee to the level of every day's
> Most quiet need, by sun and candle light.
> I love thee freely, as men strive for Right;
> I love thee purely, as they turn from Praise.
> I love thee with the passion put to use
> In my old griefs, and with my childhood's faith.
> I love thee with a love I seemed to lose
> With my lost saints—I love thee with the breath,
> Smiles, tears, of all my life!—and, if God choose,
> I shall but love thee better after death.[9]

Elizabeth died in 1861 when she was fifty-five years old and Robert forty-nine, after only fifteen years of marriage. He never remarried, but continued to immortalize her in his own poems.

Rummaging through the library here at Regent's Park College, I found a fascinating essay that the Reverend J. J. G. Graham, an Oxonian, prepared for reading before a meeting of the Browning Society on June 28, 1889, the year of Robert's death. Entitled "The Wife-love and Friend-love of Robert Browning," the essay cites the passages where Robert pays tributes of affection to Elizabeth again and again and tributes to his intimate friendships with others through the years.[10] Examples follow.

9. *Oxford Dictionary of Quotations*, 2d ed. (London: Oxford University, 1953, 1959), p. 88.
10. Found in *Browning Studies*, ed. Edward Berdoe (London: George Allen, 1895), pp. 204ff.

Robert's poem "One Word More," with the notation "To E. B. B.,
London, September, 1855" is utterly given to his love for Elizabeth.
One needs to read the entire poem to feel completely their closeness,
but the following lines reflect his heart for her. The poem is a dedication to his wife of the collection of poems entitled *Men and Women*:

> There they are, my fifty men and women
> Naming me the fifty poems finished!
> Take them, love, the book and me together:
> Where the heart lies, let the brain lie also.

Browning had verse and nothing else to offer his wife:

> I shall never, in the years remaining,

[and they were to be only six, unfortunately]

> Paint you pictures, no, nor carve you statues,
> Make you music that should all-express me;
> So it seems: I stand on my attainment.
> This of verse alone, one life allows me;
> Verse and nothing else have I to give you.
> Other heights in other lives, God willing:
> All the gifts from all the heights, your own, love!

Or, who can forget that hidden invitation to Elizabeth?

> Grow old along with me!
> The best is yet to be,
> The last of life, for which the first was made:
> Our times are in His hand
> Who saith, 'A whole I planned,
> Youth shows but half; trust God; see all, nor be afraid!'
> ["Rabbi be Ezra," St. 1]

Moreover, Browning's warm heart reached out to several close
friends:

> I love, am loved by
> Some few honest to the core.

Browning seems to have been

> the proper
> Friend-making, everywhere friend-finding soul.

In the dedications of several of his works, he expressed deep and intimate friendship for such well-known people as Thomas Carlyle and Alfred Lord Tennyson.[11] We will all be eternally indebted to the Brownings for their beautifully written insights into intimacy, both in marriage and in friendships.

Commitment: A Basic Requirement

To reach and remain on the intimacy level calls for a basic requirement: commitment. I mean by this commitment to the other person in the dyad and commitment to maintaining the depth and closeness of the relationship.

Commitment refers to a person's avowed intention to maintain a relationship by personal loyalty, trust, and mutuality in thoughts, feelings, and experiences. One of the most inspiring and moving expressions of this kind of commitment is found in the Bible. It is not the expression of a husband and wife or of a parent and child, but of a young widow, Ruth, for her mother-in-law, Naomi.

> But Ruth replied, "Don't urge me to leave you or to turn back from you. Where you go I will go, and where you stay I will stay. Your people will be my people and your God my God. Where you die I will die, and there I will be buried. May the LORD deal with me, be it ever so severely, if anything but death separates you and me. [Ruth 1:16–17, NIV]

Commitment to developing intimacy involves making investments of time, emotion, and physical energy. You are willing to be seen with, known as a close friend of, and identified with the other person at whatever the social cost. Commitment includes focusing upon each other to the possible exclusion of others at certain times.

Therefore, intimacy does not come accidentally or casually. It happens when two or more people are willing to pay the necessary price and work diligently to reach this deepest of levels.

The Four Loves and Intimacy

Ancient Greek literature includes four words for love, a study of which may help us understand better the level of intimacy. The noted British writer C. S. Lewis devoted an entire book to his study of these words.[12]

11. Ibid., pp. 217–18.
12. C. S. Lewis, *The Four Loves* (New York: Harcourt Brace Jovanovich, 1971). See also C. E. B. Cranfield, "Love," in *A Theological Word Book of the Bible*, ed. Alan Richardson (London: SCM, 1957), pp. 131–36.

The first of these words is *storgē*, which can be translated "love" or "affection." It describes especially the affection between parents and children. It is rarely used to convey the idea of sexual love.

Another word is *erōs*, which can be translated "sensual love" or "desire" (with the idea of sexual passion). This implies that there is a sense of worth or value in the loved object and that one desires to possess and enjoy this object. *Erōs* is primarily egocentric, seeking its object for the sake of its own satisfaction, fulfillment, and enhancement.

A third word is *philia*, which is friendly love, filial love, social love, affectionate regard, fondness, or friendship. This noun was often used to suggest family affections, especially between brothers and sisters.

The fourth term is *agapē*, which is used in the Bible to describe God's love for man and man's love for God. This is the highest kind of love wherein one loves sacrificially with no expected return. It is love for even the unlovely and undeserving. It is total, unconditional love. This is love that flows more out of the will than the emotions. The word *agapē* conveys the idea of a love that shows itself by helping its object rather than desiring to possess and enjoy it. This describes Hosea's love for his wayward wife, Gomer, and the love of the husband for his bride in the Song of Songs (in the Septuagint). This is redemptive love: it forgives, transforms, unconditionally accepts, makes new, infuses new life, restores, saves, and reconciles.

All four forms of love are needed. Without *erōs* we would not have been born. Without *storgē* we would not have been reared. Without *philia* we would have no friends. Without *agapē* we would not know God nor His salvation, and there would be no Christian life.

On the deeper levels of relating, *erōs* has its place in the sexual dimension of marriage, *storgē* in the warmth of family life, and *philia* in all relationships involving friendship, whereas *agapē* transforms all levels into a spiritual experience of sacrificial giving of oneself at the point of others' needs. The intimacy level provides for the deepest expression of all four forms of love.[13]

<hr>

13. For important scholarly treatments of the topic of love, see Victor P. Furnish, *The Love Command in the New Testament* (Nashville: Abingdon, 1972); James Moffatt, *Love in the New Testament* (London: Hodder and Stoughton, 1929); Anders Nygren, *Agape and Eros*, trans. Philip Watson (Chicago: University of Chicago, 1982); Gene Outka, *Agape: An Ethical Analysis*, Publications in Religion series, no. 17 (New Haven: Yale University, 1972); and Pheme Perkins, *Love Commands in the New Testament* (New York: Paulist Press, 1982).

11

Ways to Reach the Deeper Levels

"How do you get there?" a British pastor asked me at lunch when I told him that I was writing about deepening one's relationships. "I know that I need and want to develop deeper friendships," he continued, "but tell us how to do it." In this chapter I will attempt to describe some ways to reach the deeper levels.

Most of you are already relating to several if not many people on levels 1–5. Many of these relationships are casual, occasional, and in many cases fleeting. From time to time you may have had a taste of experiencing levels 6–8. Some of you have never been past level 5. I am assuming that, because you've read this far, you want to develop the deeper relationships and sustain them.

A Map for the Journey

For an American, traveling in Britain absolutely requires a map. I grew up in southwestern Oklahoma where our forefathers laid out most of the roads on a true north-south, east-west grid. But in Britain the roads were planned on the basis of trails made by animals and confused people centuries ago! On cloudy days in Oxfordshire I have no sense of direction whatsoever. I have come to appreciate a map.

169

By analogy, to reach the deeper levels of relating, one also needs a map. I have already spelled out several instructions for our map in previous chapters as I explained each level. The main points were the desired destinations. If you don't know where you're going, you'll certainly never get there. Explaining the deeper levels clarifies our objectives.

Without a map it's possible for one to not even know that there are other destinations. Some people never leave where they are. They never go any further because they have no idea of what's down the road. For example, in 1974 we were on our way to Dallas from Florida and discovered that the muffler on our car was coming loose. We pulled off the freeway in southern Louisiana to find a service station but had to angle off about three miles on a road to the nearest town. The station we found was at an intersection of a Y, and it looked like we could take the opposite road back to the freeway and save a couple of miles. After the station attendant fixed the muffler, I asked him, "Would it be possible to take this road to the right and get back on the freeway, rather than taking the road on the left we had taken to leave the freeway, since we're going on west?" The elderly local man gazed down the road on the right for a few moments as he took off his hat and scratched his head. Then finally he replied in all seriousness, "Well sah, you can try!"

Well, we tried and made it, saving the extra couple of miles, but I couldn't help wonder about that old fellow back at the station. He had no idea what was down the road only three miles from where he worked and lived. And the sad thing about it was that he really didn't want to know. He was satisfied to live in his limited world of about one square mile. There are a lot of people like him living on level 4 or 5.

A map is both an encouragement and an invitation to travel. It is helpful in showing us the way to specific destinations. But it is also proof that others have made the journey. The very fact that someone has made a map shows that it is both possible and worthwhile to make the journey. In the same way, I want you to know that it is both possible and worthwhile to develop deep relationships.

Deepening one's relationships is like taking a journey. Do you recall the Alley Oop cartoons of the 1930s and 1940s? You could step into Dr. Wungum's Time Machine and be transported instantly to another point in time. Instant time travel sounds exciting, but that doesn't work in relationships. You have to travel step by step, mile by mile.

I'm talking about a kind of *Pilgrim's Progress* in developing relationships. It's a process, it takes time, and the goals are out in front to be reached. You have to keep moving.

The journey is full of pitfalls, obstacles, problems, detours, washouts, and difficulties of all kinds. Not everyone will want to go with you. Your journey will be threatening to some of your present so-called friends. They will think you are getting too personal. They may even think you have become "strange." Some will not prove trustworthy. Others will back away and desert you. Some of your efforts at going deeper may precipitate conflict with those who are insecure and easily intimidated.

However, it is a journey with many benefits and joys that make the travel worth every effort. You will find that the caring, the sharing, and the intimacy add color, excitement, richness, and joy to life.

As you plan and begin your journey, remember that the initiative is yours. No one else can do this for you. Decide where you want to go by determining what is the deepest level of relating you are experiencing. If you're not really caring about someone, then select some people who need you to care about them. What needs to be done? Make a list of goals that are reasonable and attainable. Then make yourself available.

If you're already on the caring level but not the sharing level, start with one or two of your best friends and begin opening up to them. Follow the suggestions in chapter 9 with regard to self-disclosure. Start with your closest friend before moving on to a second.

I also suggest that you gain some experience on the caring and sharing levels before moving to level 8. When you're ready for intimacy, start with your mate or best friend. A married person ought not develop an intimate relationship with someone else and leave his or her mate behind, unless of course the mate wants it that way. In that case, relate on this level with people of your own sex to avoid complications in the marriage.

If you're single, start with your best friend and develop the quality of friendship you both desire. In time, include others. People who relate on the deeper levels tend to attract others to join them. Set clear goals and pursue them.

Apply the principles of relating on the deeper levels. Review chapters 8, 9, and 10. Develop your awareness. Find or create specific ways to get involved in other people's lives. Begin taking leaps of faith with some selected friends. Open yourself up to them. Run the risks. Be honest. Loosen up and be yourself. Discover the meaning of love. Become a toucher, but keep your motives pure. Reach out and some will respond. Remain flexible. Be patient. Work on your own maturity and growth. Get freed up, laid back, and relaxed. Do what you know to do best and what the situation warrants, and in the meantime ask and depend upon God to lead you and make it happen. God is in the business of bringing people closer together. As you draw closer to Him, He will draw others closer to you and you to them. These are some of the principles to use in moving deeper.

Although the main responsibility for developing deeper relationships belongs to you and depends upon your initiative and cooperation with God's efforts, my experience convinces me that one very good way to travel on this journey is with a group. Most of us work better with groups than we do alone. For one thing, we are more motivated if we have someone to whom we are responsible—whether it be an individual or a group.

Relationships require others. Why not develop the deeper levels with a committed and responsible group that is seeking common goals? I have referred earlier in this book to our use of small groups in our church in Los Alamos. There are several different ways to do this. In *The Wounded Parent* I discuss in detail the use of a small group as a support system for hurting parents.[1] The dynamics could also apply to people seeking growth in relationships. Refer to the list of suggested readings at the end of chapter 9 for further information.

If your church doesn't have anything like a small-group ministry, then start one of your own. Use this book as a starter. Invite a half dozen or so friends over to your home and propose that the group meet one night a week to study a chapter a week. Rotate the sessions among the homes of the participants. Each person should have his or her own copy (for marking up and note-taking) to read in advance of each session. Designate a different person in the group to lead the discussion. Notice I say *discussion.* Don't teach the book page by page. Let the members participate. Agree to meet for two hours, or at least an hour and a half. Although some may wish to linger and talk, let others feel free to leave at the end of the set time.

At the end of twelve weeks you will be ready to evaluate the experience and suggest future plans. The group may wish to terminate, or

1. Guy Greenfield, *The Wounded Parent: Coping with Parental Discouragement* (Grand Rapids: Baker, 1982), pp. 109–19.

it may wish to become a regular prayer-and-share group, or a prayer-and-care group dealing with specific projects of need in the church or community. Always inform your pastor about what you're doing in this regard. Let him know of your intentions (give him a copy of this book). Invite his prayers and encouragement. It may be important for him to know you're not starting a holier-than-thou club of supersaints to sit in judgment upon the other church members. Remember that one of your goals is to become nurturers.

Finally, I have found that people generally travel faster in groups. The mutual encouragement and stimulation experienced in a small group of friends who meet each week to pray, share, and study together far exceed that experienced in traveling alone in most cases.

Paying the Price for Developing Deep Relationships

Are you willing to pay the price for developing deep relationships? Oil-company drillers have found that to drill at thirty thousand feet instead of ten thousand feet is very expensive. Until the price of oil went up a few years ago, many felt they couldn't afford to drill deeper. But they knew that in many cases you don't strike oil at the shallower levels.

Reaching deeper levels of relating takes time and is costly. If you're too busy to develop closeness, then you're too busy. To meet with a group of committed friends one night a week, for example, requires setting that evening aside and foregoing something else. Taking your wife out one evening a week to dinner, the theater, or the park takes time and possibly money you would not have spent otherwise.

It takes energy and effort to care for people in need, to spend time with your friends, and to share yourself with others. If you're not satisfied or gaining a sense of fulfillment in your current relationships, then you're probably not investing much of yourself in them. You get what you pay for. In the summer of 1965, Robert McCracken, then pastor of the Riverside Church in New York City, told me that Harry Emerson Fosdick, his well-known predecessor, was having the time of his life in those last years of his retirement: working several hours a week in a rescue mission in one of New York's toughest neighborhoods. Fosdick's theology was liberal, but his caring for people in need was magnanimous. Greatness always expresses itself in caring. But caring will cost you.

However, look at the other side of going deeper: staying where you

are on the shallower levels. Now that's really expensive! Think of the
price one pays in distant relationships: loneliness, drabness, triviality
in living, lack of excitement, and superficial interests. That's the highest price of all to pay!

A quick survey of the rewards found at the deeper levels convinces
almost anyone that the efforts expended are worth it. For example,
there is a lot of giving done on the caring level: time, energy, money,
yourself, love. Anyone who has done any of this consistently will agree
with the words of Jesus, "It is more blessed to give than to receive"
(Acts 20:35, NIV). Paul told us that "God loves a cheerful giver" (2 Cor.
9:7b, NIV). Well, I do too. As a matter of fact, anyone who has reached
the caring level on a consistent basis will be a cheerful giver. Such
caring givers are always cheerful. They have discovered the joys of
giving.

You will find a lot of love on the deeper levels. It comes in the
reciprocation within the friendships you create. Caring produces caring. Sharing produces sharing. Intimacy reproduces itself. As you love
and accept others on these levels, so you will be loved and accepted
in return.

The most valuable possessions you own are your friends. You cannot
buy friends; they must be created through the avenues of caring and
sharing. This makes their value permanent, not subject to economic
trends of depression or inflation. It was Lord Byron who described the
permanence of friends when he penned,

> Friendship is Love without his wings![2]

Or who can forget Robert Browning's exclamation?

> You're my friend—
> What a thing friendship is, world without end![3]

Deep friendships, moreover, bring support, encouragement, and affirmation, by which one can face anything. Have you ever faced the
loss of a loved one, your spouse, a child, or one of your parents? Who
were the first to come? Who stayed the longest? Who came back even

2. "Hours of Idleness. L'Amitie," in the *Oxford Dictionary of Quotations*, 2d ed.
(London: Oxford University, 1953, 1959), p. 91.
3. "The Flight of the Duchess," st. 17, in the *Oxford Dictionary of Quotations*, p. 117.

days after the funeral? Your closest friends. We all need to learn all we can about developing friendships.[4]

A most significant benefit of living on the deeper levels is personal growth. You learn a great deal about yourself, about God, and about living. You change, and for the better. You become more sensitive to the needs of others. You become a better listener. You discover strengths you never knew you had. You develop a more positive self-image. You find a measure of inner peace that you never knew on the shallower levels. Yes, the rewards make the effort worth it.

New Levels of Awareness

I trust that by now, as you've been reading this book, you are discovering new levels of awareness about yourself.

Are you aware of where you are with those you consider your friends and associates, relatives and companions, at this time in your life? At what level are you with each of them? That is to ask, what is the maximum level of depth that you and each of these ever reach?

It might help to take a sheet of paper and list the twenty or thirty most important people in your life, people you see once or more a week at least. Include friends or relatives who live at a distance geographically if you either write to or telephone them once a week. Take a few moments to think about each one. In one column to the right of the list, write down the number of the deepest level of relating you have attained and are sustaining with some regularity with each person. Don't be in any hurry with this. Take time to evaluate as accurately as possible.

Now, in a second column further to the right of each name, write down the number(s) of the level you would like to achieve in the future with each person on the list. Also, consider what the will of God might be in these relationships. This number should be the level of not only what is desired but also what is reasonable, attainable, and practical in view of the fact that the deeper the levels, the fewer the people you can relate to meaningfully.

Here is a hypothetical list:

---

4. The best book about friendship that I have read is Alan Loy McGinnis's *The Friendship Factor* (Minneapolis: Augsburg, 1979). The author is a Christian counseling psychologist.

Name	Current Level	Future Level
Mary (wife)	6	7, 8
Bill	5	6, 7
Sue	4	5
Jim	2	4

Such a list will give you some goals toward which you may aim. The more specifically you can deal with setting priorities for deepening your relationships, the better. You usually go nowhere with vague generalities. Thinking about levels of relating and doing something specific about attaining them may be two different things.

After you work through the list of names, ask how the eight levels of relating fit into your life experiences. Look over your list. How deep are you now with *anyone*? What is the deepest level you now reach? If you're married and you're not on levels 6, 7, or 8 with your husband or wife, why not? Have you simply not been aware of these specific levels for relating with him or her, or are there some emotional, mental, experiential, or spiritual barriers? If it is the former, can you invite him or her to a study of the possibilities (by reading this book, if nothing else)? Would he or she cooperate? If the problem is one of the barriers, can you identify what it is, analyze it, and get some help to remove it?

If you're single, at what level are you now with your closest friend of either sex? Are you on levels 6, 7, or 8? If not, is it a matter of a lack of awareness or some barrier? Do you see what needs to be done in order to go deeper?

How deep are you willing to go with those you now know best? Are there fears or reservations that you have that need to be examined?

Ideally, all eight levels should be found in everyone's experiences of relating. Currently, I am trying to operate on all eight levels with people in my life. Most of these relationships are on the shallower levels. I simply do not have time to even speak to all the people I see each day (level 1). I can greet a good many as we pass on the street, sidewalk, or in the halls of buildings where we meet (level 2). I can converse with some of those I greet and get acquainted with them. Many of these I will discover have separate interests from mine (level 3), while even fewer will have common interests with me (level 4). Both the former and the latter offer me new experiences and a pool of potential friends for the future. Even fewer will be those with whom I will participate in some activity at church, home, or work (level 5).

These will be the people I may casually refer to in polite conversation as my friends, while those on levels 3 and 4 are acquaintances.

Even fewer will be the people for whom I will care in some tangible way (level 6). I will try to get involved in their lives to meet specific perceived needs. Then even fewer will be my closest friends with whom I openly and freely share my inner feelings, attitudes, experiences and subsequent interpretations (level 7). This will be a relationship where reciprocation follows. Finally, I will have a very few, maybe only one or two, people with whom I relate on an intimate basis where our communications are quite personal (level 8).

Moreover, depending upon circumstances and times, I may relate to a specific person (I will use the example of my wife) on all eight levels in the course of a week. There may be an occasion when I will avoid her (level 1) because I will be angry with her over something; at other times we will simply greet each other (level 2) and go on with our separate responsibilities around the house or as we go off to work; at other times we may discuss some separate interests (level 3) as we plan the weekend, but eventually agree on some common interests (level 4) as possible activities. At other times we may participate in some common activity (cleaning the house, working in the garden, going to church; level 5).

At other times, I may perceive some specific need in her life (she wants to cook dinner but simply feels too tired to do so) and get involved to the extent that the need is met (I cook dinner for her or take her out to eat; level 6). At other times the two of us will sit in the patio swing and share our deepest feelings about some common or personal concerns (level 7). The sharing may be positive or negative but "it's who I am right now." Finally, there will be those tender moments of affection—touching, crying, or laughing—when we have our deepest sharing (level 8). It may be in the car riding down the freeway when never a word is spoken between us, or walking in the cool breeze of an evening in the park, or at night in bed before we fall asleep.

It is my conviction that relating to some people on the deeper levels inevitably enriches my relationships on all levels. I am a better, happier, more enjoyable person to relate to on any of the levels with all the people I see because I am drawing strength from the deeper relationships and have developed the lifestyle of one who nurtures rather than one who judges or criticizes.

After I shared these ideas with a church group on a retreat, one older woman with many years of experience with all kinds of people commented in a discussion period, "Well, I have noticed that people who have a few friends at the deeper levels have more meaningful relationships at the other levels." I couldn't have said it better.

You have read enough by now to see where you are and where you might want to be in the eight levels of relating. To fail to act now will probably mean you'll stay right where you are. If you truly want to grow, I strongly suggest you start *now*. Start somewhere with someone.

12

Motivation for Ethics
at the Deeper Levels

Most people will say that they want to live right, do what is right, and be moral and upright in all their behavior. Christians in particular will generally claim that they desire to do the will of God and live by the teachings of the Bible and especially of Jesus. Whatever one claims as the highest moral standards and however much one tries to live up to those standards, one rarely asks why. "Why not simply do as I please and everybody else go and jump in the river? It's my life and I'll do as I please! You do your thing, and I'll do mine."

Well, a lot of people live that way. Thirty minutes of driving in freeway traffic will convince anyone of that. But most people try to do what they believe is in the best interests of themselves and everyone else, and they generally call this doing the right thing. Why do they try to do what is right? Because they were taught to do the right, and they were taught well? Because of fear of doing wrong and being punished?

No. I believe that people generally act out of a response to other people, out of the quality of their interpersonal relationships. When those relationships are wholesome, meaningful, and rewarding, their behavior tends to be cooperative, law-abiding, and benevolent, if not altruistic. Their professed religious faith may or may not have any-

179

thing to do with the way they behave. Most behavior and attitudes[1] flow out of the nature of one's relationships with the significant others in one's life.

How does all of this relate to the Christian life? What is distinctive in the Christian faith that makes a unique difference in one's behavior and attitudes? This chapter is an attempt to answer these questions.

The Meaning of Ethics

The term *ethics* is relatively new to many people who are not acquainted with academic terminology. About all they ever hear on the subject is the news coverage dealing with a congressional or legislative ethics committee's investigation of one of our public servant's unethical behavior, which usually has to do with cheating or stealing. Basically, ethics is a systematic study or discipline concerning what people *ought to do* in the light of some standard of behavior. This standard will reflect a set of values regarding behavior that society generally considers proper.

Ethical standards may be rooted in custom, law, religion, or a mix of all three. A standard of ethics sets forth guidelines for how people should behave. An example would be: "People should be honest, fair, and true in all dealings (business or otherwise) with one another." Consequently, it would be wrong to cheat or steal. Fraud, conspiracy, or deception would be unethical. Why? Because the recognized authority (custom, law, or religion) says so. Originally, the authority may have set the standard because it was obvious that dishonesty was harmful in its consequences. In time, the original reason for the standard may be forgotten, but the standard is still upheld by virtue of the authority behind it.

Values are those ideas, beliefs, traits, virtues, goals, or objects that a people recognize as having worth and are, therefore, worth pursuing and living by. Behind all ethical standards lie certain values (e.g., freedom, honesty, truth, integrity, life, sexual fidelity, health, cleanliness, democracy, money, property). The biblical word for value is "the good." Behind every biblical command is a value that reflects something of the nature, character, or will of God. The command *thou shalt not kill* reflects the value of human life, for man is made in the image of God.

---

1. Behavior: way of conducting oneself; moral conduct, treatment of others. Attitudes: settled way of thinking; disposition of opinion.

Christian ethics is a systematic study of the sense of oughtness that flows out of one's relationship with God through Jesus Christ in the context of both biblical revelation and a community of faith, involving both being and doing, and expressed both individually and socially. Christian ethics is a careful study of what is involved in living the Christian life in all of its dimensions, combining an emphasis upon both motives and consequent behavior. There are eight elements involved in understanding Christian ethics.

1. *A systematic study*: ethics is an intellectual examination that is no substitute for living the Christian life itself. As biology and chemistry are related to medicine, so is Christian ethics related to Christian living. Theory precedes application in its finest expression.

2. *A sense of oughtness*: ethics has to do with an awareness of right and wrong, righteousness (justice) and sin, good and evil, and a sense of obligation to do the right based upon the will of God as it informs one's conscience.

3. *An expression of one's relationship with God*: Christian ethics is for Christians only. The Christian life is reflective of the new life from God that flows out of one's personal relationship with God. Christian ethics is theological ethics. It is not based upon human reason or merely humanistic concerns. It is a study of human conduct as determined by divine conduct, to use Emil Brunner's phrase.

4. *Through Jesus Christ*: the Christian's supreme knowledge of God is revealed through Jesus Christ, God's Son. Christian ethics is Christ-centered and based upon the teachings of Jesus and His apostles. It is not merely religious ethics but rather ethics based upon the early *Christian* tradition. The Christian life is the life of Jesus Christ being lived in and through the believer.

5. *In the context of biblical revelation*: Christian ethics is based upon the teachings of the Bible. Its principles are those revealed in the infallible Scriptures of the Christian faith as passed down through the centuries by the church.

6. *In the context of a community of faith*: Christian ethics is in and for the church of Jesus Christ. It is a church-centered ethic. Christian ethical decisionmaking has not only the insights of the Bible and the guidance of the Holy Spirit but also the collective resources of a local congregation of believers and their past heritage to give direction for right action.

7. *Involving both being and doing*: Christian ethics seeks to maintain a balance between character development in the likeness of Christ and

good works or deeds, performed in the name of Christ, which reflect
the kind of actions He was known for.

8. Expressed both individually and socially: Christian ethics calls for
the individual believer to focus upon not only the growth of individual
Christian character (whose foundation is a new birth experience of
salvation) but also a collective or social responsibility in and to the
institutions of society.

However, what motivates the Christian to live the Christian life?

The Need for Motivation

The motivation for living the Christian life comes from several
sources.

First, there must be *new life* itself. The Christian life is not a human
life that is merely imitating the life of Jesus as it is reflected in the
pages of the New Testament. That would be an impossibility. The well-
known novel by Charles Sheldon, *In His Steps*, subtitled *What Would
Jesus Do?* reflects the idea that imitating Jesus is the heart of the
gospel. This misses the point of the New Testament—that one needs
to be born again (John 3:3–7) and be made alive, afresh, and anew
within one's heart in order to produce the works of God (Eph. 2:1–10).
Christian life is not a reformed old life but a new creation and a God-
given righteousness (right standing before God; 2 Cor. 5:17–21). Christ
Himself indwelling the heart of the believer is the Christian's new life
(Col. 3:1–4). Christ is present through the Holy Spirit (2 Cor. 3:17–18;
Gal. 5:22–25) living in and through the believer.

Second, Christians are motivated by biblical instruction and by
both the private and corporate worship of God. The Bible teaches me
who I am, *what* I am, and what I ought to *be* and *do*. There is motivation in knowing the truth of God about what He has done for me
and what He wants to do in and through my life. There is an inherent
motivation in this kind of information provided from the powerful
Word of God (Heb. 4:11–13). The entire 119th Psalm (all 176 verses!)
describes such motivation. Moreover, worship provides an immediate
sense of awareness of the presence of God Himself. Such awareness
always motivates: "Here am I. Send me!" (see Isa. 6:1–8, NIV).

But is this the whole story? I believe not. A close examination of
the New Testament reveals that relationships were a major force for
ethical motivation in the lives of the early Christians. Therefore, the
new life needs both information and motivation. Neither is inherent

within it. Merely *knowing* the right is no guarantee of *doing* the right. Worship not only raises the believer's awareness of the presence of God but also gathers believers together into a body of relationships that provide the motivation to do the right.

The relationships described in the New Testament records of the first Christians are largely those on the deeper levels: caring, sharing, and intimacy. It is my very strong conviction, therefore, that *only at these deeper levels of relating will Christians discover the necessary dynamic for living the Christian life in its fullness.*

The earliest Christians greeted each other, met and discussed their separate and common interests, and socially interacted, but they went on to the deeper levels of caring, sharing, and intimacy within the small house churches and in their families. Their fellowship was deep and abiding. These Christians were like a close-knit family. They called themselves brothers and sisters and called God their Father. They were a constant stimulus to each other to live the Christian life. Their love for each other was of the deepest and closest kind.

Christian ethics provides the moral direction for the life of the Christian, but it is the quality and depth of the believer's relationships (with both God and one's fellow believers) that provide the motivation for living that life. The early Christians were not a collection of individual believers following Jesus each in his or her own way and place, but a fellowship, a family, a congregation, and a body of disciples following Jesus *together*. So it must be in every generation of the church.

The Connection of Faith, Ethics, and Behavior

Why is an emphasis on behavior for the Christian so important? Isn't it enough simply to believe the Bible and the basic doctrines of the Christian faith? If you believe "the five fundamentals" of evangelical Christianity (although the more I study the Bible and listen to the Holy Spirit teach me, the longer my list of "fundamentals" becomes), won't behavior take care of itself?[2] Unfortunately, there is a prevailing mentality of this sort throughout a large segment of evangelical Christianity today.

2. The "five fundamentals" are the virgin birth of Jesus, the bodily resurrection of Jesus, the inerrancy (infallibility) of the Scriptures, the substitutionary theory of atonement (Jesus' death on the cross), and the imminent, physical second coming of Jesus. See Wayne Ward, "Fundamentalism," in *Encyclopedia of Southern Baptists*, 2 vols. (Nashville: Broadman, 1958), vol. 1, pp. 515–16.

The Bible teaches that one's behavior is *crucial*. It is the real test of the validity of one's faith. Jesus taught that there is a close connection among faith, ethics, and behavior. Ethics is the other side of the "faith coin"; behavior shows whether the coin is genuine or not. An orthodox profession of faith ("Lord, Lord," Matt. 7:21–23) is in itself insufficient. Even performing marvelous, charismatic, and sensational works won't make up for the absence of the ethical dimension.

Jesus put it this way: "Not everyone who says to me, 'Lord, Lord,' will enter the kingdom of heaven, but only he who does the will of my Father who is in heaven. Many will say to me on that day, 'Lord, Lord, did we not prophesy in your name, and in your name drive out demons and perform many miracles?' Then will I tell them plainly, 'I never knew you. Away from me, you evildoers!' " (Matt. 7:21–23, NIV). In the verses following these Jesus stressed both hearing and *doing* His words as the proper foundation of one's life (Matt. 7:24–27). Actually, the entire Sermon on the Mount is an exposition of the connection of faith, ethics, and behavior.

Further into Matthew's Gospel, when Jesus was teaching about the final judgment, He clearly stated that the criterion for God's judgment of people will not be a simple checkup on one's orthodoxy of faith but the testing of the quality of one's *behavior:* feeding the hungry, giving drink to the thirsty, welcoming the stranger, clothing the naked, and visiting the imprisoned (Matt. 25:31–46).

One's behavior toward others is one's behavior toward Jesus Himself: "Whatever you did (or, did not do) for one of the least of these brothers of mine, you did (or, did not do) for me" (compare Matt. 25:40 and 45, NIV). One's faith relationship to Jesus is validated by and revealed in one's behavior.

Both Paul and Peter warned that in the last days false prophets would abound. How would they be identified? By their unorthodox theology? Such would be evident, but the real clues would be their *behavior*: immoral, unethical, arrogant, self-centered, materialistic, and empty of love for others (read 2 Tim. 3:1–9; 2 Peter 2). Numerous other passages from Scripture could be marshaled to illustrate further the connection of faith, ethics, and behavior (e.g., Eph. 2:8–10; Gal. 5:6; James 2:14–26).

Please don't misunderstand me. One's theology or doctrinal belief is also crucial. Witness the rise of all sorts of non-Christian sects and cults in the Western world over the past 150 years. Witness the weakening of major denominations by a debilitating theological liberalism that attempts to strip the Bible of its power by elevating human reason above divine revelation; human reason in turn rationalizes all biblical teaching into culturally conditioned uncertainties. Such rational scepticism invariably produces unbelief.

The Great Commission of Jesus to His disciples clearly sets forth this balance: "Therefore go and make disciples . . . teaching them to *obey* everything I have commanded you. And surely I will be with you always, to the very end of the age" (Matt. 28:19–20, NIV; italics added). Notice here the connection among *faith* ("make disciples"), *ethics* ("teaching them"), and *behavior* ("to obey").

Discouragement and Relational Deficiency

Relational deficiency results when persons rarely if ever develop relationships beyond level 5, social interaction. The evidence of relational deficiency is a judgmental, critical, and negative spirit toward others. But something else can happen: discouragement and lack of motivation to live up to one's ethical standards, especially under stress or during emotional turmoil.

If this is true of people generally, why should it not be equally true of Christians? Now let's be honest. Christians who do not go beyond level 5 have certain motivations to live by the teachings of the Bible: gratitude to God, the guidance and promptings of the indwelling Holy Spirit, the instruction of the biblical teachings themselves, an enlightened and active conscience, fear of punishment for doing wrong, expectation of rewards for doing right, and social pressure from fellow believers (a kind of moral accountability to them). Yet most of these can wane and falter as time goes by and unusual pressures or stresses develop in one's life. We can forget, grow careless and indifferent, and lose touch with God and others. Then what?

The lack of relating to others on levels 6, 7, and 8 can make a Christian a prime target for discouragement. When you are not caring or being cared for, when you are not sharing your innermost self with a few confidants who understand, when there is no intimacy with anyone in your life, *watch out!* The resulting relational deficiency will create a real letdown when you experience sufficient stress: persistent illness (your own or that of a family member), financial reversals, death of a loved one, betrayal by apparent friends, loss of a job, sexual frustrations, excessive responsibilities at work, long absences from home due to one's job, ongoing conflict with children, to name only a few pressures.

Rudolf Dreikurs, child psychiatrist and author, taught that a misbehaving child tended to be a discouraged child.[3] I believe that this
principle applies to people of all ages. A misbehaving adult tends to
be a discouraged adult.

Of the hundreds of people I have counseled over the past thirty
years or so, with few exceptions those who were tangled in various
sorts of immoral behavior were primarily *discouraged* people. Some
of that discouragement was the result of their wrong behavior, to be
sure. Sin is never an encouraging experience. But their case histories
revealed that a related cause of their misbehavior and, I believe, a
major factor in the early stages of their difficulties was a great deal of
discouragement somewhere in their interpersonal relationships with
the significant others in their lives.

I have never counseled a Christian involved in some kind of extramarital affair who was not already discouraged in his or her marriage
when the affair began. I have had no way of empirically testing this,
but I also strongly suspect that none of these people had ever, except
on rare occasions, discovered the deeper levels (6, 7, and 8) of relating.
Although each one of them was responsible for what was clearly wrong
behavior, all were also victims of relational deficiency.

Encouragement and Relational Sufficiency

Relational sufficiency is the consequence of people maintaining some
or several relationships with people on the deeper levels of caring,
sharing, and intimacy. The evidences of relational sufficiency are a
nurturing, affirming, and positive spirit toward others. However,
something else happens: a person will find a constant source of encouragement and motivation to live up to his or her ethical standards,
especially under stress or during emotional turmoil.

Again, let's be honest. As Christians we need more than the Bible,
church instruction and activities, prayer, a sound evangelical theology,
a hard-working and prodding conscience, threats of punishment and
promises of reward, and pressure from fellow believers at church to
do what's right in daily living. *We need each other* in some meaningful
relationships at the deeper levels.

I am not talking about the "cheery support" of a few close friends
or the idea that there is someone to come and hold my hand during

3. Rudolf Dreikurs and Vicki Soltz, *Children: The Challenge* (New York: Hawthorn,
1964), pp. 36ff.

a bout with depression. I am talking about a sustained sense of self-worth made possible by a steady involvement in the lives of needy people, by reciprocal experiences of trust through consistent self-disclosure to loving confidants, and by a growing sense of togetherness with one or more intimate friends.

When I know that I am of infinite value to God, to others, and to myself, then there will well up from within me the strength to face the living of any day. This inner strength is the constant encouragement and motivation to live up to the ethical demands of the Christian faith as revealed in Scripture and in the context of the church's life.

The Dynamics of the Deeper Levels

God provides the motivation for the Christian to behave in a Christ-like manner. Such motivation is the power to put Christian principles or ethics into practice. In one sense I can say that the Christian life is Jesus Christ living in and through me. In another sense I can say that God expects me to be obedient to Him in doing His will. I can know the will of God from reading the Bible, exercising my reason in understanding it, seeking the moral guidance of other believers in the church and in history, and depending upon the Holy Spirit to reveal, illuminate, and guide as I use the Bible in decisionmaking.

However, *knowing* the will of God in specific situations or in facing certain decisions and *wanting to do* the will of God may be two different realities. Again, God provides the will to do, but I believe that He largely does this *through* people in our lives to whom we are close. My relationships with others on the deeper levels are where God motivates me to actualize the ethics of my Christian faith. This is the power to put principles into practice. God works through the people for whom I care, the people with whom I share, and those who are closest to me to motivate my actions to conform to the life of Jesus Christ. Without any relationships on these levels I would flounder in Christian living. I might make a show of conforming to His example from time to time, but I would be far from reaching my potential.

The experience of caring for people in need has a kind of built-in power to motivate me to live up to the highest expectations of the people for whom I care. My caring both expresses and magnifies the ethics of my Christian faith. These ethical standards are intertwined with the way I continue to behave. The caring experience itself reinforces my commitment to these standards. Moreover, the gratitude of the people for whom I care serves as an encouragement, thus a motivation, to remain loyal to these highest ideals I call my ethics.

The experience of sharing with a few trusted confidants also reinforces my commitment to my ethics by increasing my sense of self-worth, by affirming my ethical identity (who I am and what I stand for ethically go hand in hand), and by strengthening my resolve to do what I believe to be right. The reciprocation on the part of the confidants produces the same results for them and therefore we mutually reinforce each other's behavior. If all of us in this process are Christians, it produces a binding effect in our relationships.

The experience of intimacy for the Christian takes the caring and sharing processes even deeper and with a few people, as few as one to three, provides a closeness and support that motivate one to live on the highest ethical plane possible.

Paul expressed this vividly:

> Not that I have already obtained all this, or have already been made perfect, but I press on to take hold of that for which Christ Jesus took hold of me. Brothers, I do not consider myself yet to have taken hold of it. But one thing I do: Forgetting what is behind and straining toward what is ahead, I press on toward the goal to win the prize for which God has called me heavenward in Christ Jesus.
>
> All of us who are mature should take such a view of things. And if on some point you think differently, that too God will make clear to you. Only let us live up to what we have already attained.
>
> Join with others in following my example, brothers, and take note of those who live according to the pattern we gave you. [Phil. 3:12–17, NIV]

Here Paul admitted his imperfect humanity, yet his determination to achieve God's highest potential for him shines through. The importance of relationships is evident both in these verses and throughout his letter to the Philippians. Caring (1:19–24), sharing (4:10–13), and intimacy (1:8) are all implicit in this beautiful letter. God was working through Paul's relationships with the Philippians and the Philippians' with Paul to bring about the necessary motivation to live the highest expression of the Christian life.

God is in the business of doing no less for you and me today. If you hunger for greater victory and joy in living the Christian life, you will need to deepen not only your understanding of Christian faith and ethics but also your relationships with fellow believers on the deepest levels of caring, sharing, and intimacy.

We need each other. We really do!

For Further Reading

Brister, C. W. *Take Care: Translating Christ's Love into A Caring Ministry*. Nashville: Broadman, 1978.

Carter, W. Leslie, Paul D. Meier, and Frank B. Minirth. *Why Be Lonely? A Guide to Meaningful Relationships*. Grand Rapids: Baker, 1982.

Clinebell, Howard F., Jr., and Charlotte H. Clinebell. *The Intimate Marriage*. New York: Harper and Row, 1970.

Greenfield, Guy. *The Wounded Parent: Coping with Parental Discouragement*. Grand Rapids: Baker, 1982.

Jourard, Sidney M. *The Transparent Self*. Rev. ed. New York: Van Nostrand Reinhold, 1971.

Lair, Jess. *I Ain't Well, But I Sure Am Better: Mutual Need Therapy*. New York: Doubleday, 1975.

Maston, T. B. *Why Live the Christian Life?* Nashville: Broadman, 1980.

McGinnis, Alan Loy. *The Friendship Factor*. Minneapolis: Augsburg, 1979.

Nutt, Grady. *Agaperos*. Nashville: Broadman, 1977.

Powell, John. *Why Am I Afraid to Tell You Who I Am?* Niles, IL: Argus Communications, 1969.

White, Jerry, and Mary White. *Friends and Friendship: The Secrets of Drawing Close*. Colorado Springs, CO: Navpress, 1982.